P9-CAU-507

Published by

Families Anonymous, Inc.

701 Lee Street, Suite 670
Des Plaines, IL 60016
(847) 294-5877 • fax (847) 294-5837
(800) 736-9805 (USA only)
Website: www.FamiliesAnonymous.org
E-mail: famanon@FamiliesAnonymous.org

Copyright © 1991, 2011
Families Anonymous, Inc.
All Rights Reserved
Printed in the United States of America

First edition published 1991
Revised (commemorative) edition published 2011
Current edition published 2012
Fifteenth printing since 1991

ISBN: 978-1-939168-00-9
Families Anonymous Literature Catalog #1015

TODAY

A

BETTER
WAY

TODAY A BETTER WAY

This book is dedicated to the memory of
MOOSE
whose faith and encouragement
fostered the project.

SERENITY PRAYER

God, grant me the
SERENITY to accept the things
I cannot change,
COURAGE to change the things I can, and
WISDOM to know the difference.

INTRODUCTION

TODAY A BETTER WAY provides one study page for each day of the year.

The editors thank the countless, devoted members of Families Anonymous who have contributed to this book in the form of writing, evaluating, and editing the manuscript and the galley proofs. This book could not have been produced without their sharing.

THE TWELVE STEPS
OF FAMILIES ANONYMOUS

We have found that our success in this program is determined by how well we accept and apply the following suggested Steps:

1. We admitted we were powerless over drugs and other people's lives—that *our* lives had become unmanageable.

2. Came to believe that a Power greater than ourselves could restore us to sanity.

3. Made a decision to turn our will and our lives over to the care of God *as we understood Him.*

4. Made a searching and fearless moral inventory of ourselves.

5. Admitted to God, to ourselves, and to another human being the exact nature of our wrongs.

6. Were entirely ready to have God remove all these defects of character.

7. Humbly asked Him to remove our shortcomings.

8. Made a list of all persons we had harmed, and became willing to make amends to them all.

9. Made direct amends to such people whenever possible, except when to do so would injure them or others.

10. Continued to take personal inventory, and when we were wrong, promptly admitted it.

11. Sought through prayer and meditation to improve our conscious contact with God as we understood Him, praying only for knowledge of His will for us and the power to carry that out.

12. Having had a spiritual awakening as a result of these Steps, we tried to carry this message to others and to practice these principles in all our affairs.

[Permission to use the Twelve Steps of Alcoholics Anonymous for adaptation is granted by A.A. World Services, Inc.]

THE TWELVE TRADITIONS
OF FAMILIES ANONYMOUS

We keep what we have only with vigilance. Our group experience suggests that the unity of Families Anonymous depends upon our adherence to these Traditions:

1. Our common welfare should come first; personal progress for the greatest number depends on unity.

2. For our group purpose there is but one authority—a loving God as He may express Himself in our group conscience. Our leaders are but trusted servants; they do not govern.

3. Individuals concerned with another's abuse of drugs or related problems of living, when gathered together for mutual aid, may call themselves a Families Anonymous group provided that, as a group, they have no other affiliation. The only requirement for membership is a concern about the use of mind-altering substances or related behavioral problems of a relative or friend.

4. Each group should be autonomous, except in matters affecting other groups or FA as a whole.

5. Each group has but one primary purpose: to help those concerned with someone who may have a problem of drug abuse or dependence. We do this by practicing the Twelve Steps of this program, by encouraging and understanding those affected by this illness, and by welcoming and giving comfort to the families and friends of individuals with a current, suspected, or former drug problem.

6. Our Family Groups ought never endorse, finance, or lend our name to any outside enterprise, lest problems of money, property, and prestige divert us from our primary purpose.

7. Every group ought to be fully self-supporting, declining outside contributions.

8. Families Anonymous Twelfth Step work should remain forever nonprofessional, but our service centers may employ special workers.

9. Our groups, as such, ought never be organized, but we may create service boards or committees directly responsible to those they serve.

10. Families Anonymous has no opinion on outside issues; hence our name ought never be drawn into public controversy.

11. Our public relations policy is based on attraction rather than promotion; we need always maintain personal anonymity at the level of press, radio, films, and TV. We need guard with special care the anonymity of our members, as well as those of other recovery programs.

12. Anonymity is the spiritual foundation of all our Traditions, ever reminding us to place principles above personalities.

[Permission to use the Twelve Traditions of Alcoholics Anonymous for adaptation is granted by A.A. World Services, Inc.]

THE TWELVE PROMISES
OF FAMILIES ANONYMOUS

1. We are going to know a freedom from worry and a new happiness.

2. We will not regret the past or wish to shut the door on it.

3. We will comprehend the word *serenity*.

4. We will know *peace*.

5. No matter what we've been through, we will see how our experiences can benefit others.

6. Those feelings of resentment and self-pity will disappear.

7. We will lose interest in trying to change others, and we will gain an appreciation for those special people in our lives.

8. Self-righteousness will slip away.

9. Our attitudes and our outlook on life will change.

10. Our insecurities and our fear of other people's opinions will leave us.

11. We will intuitively know how to handle situations that used to baffle us.

12. We will come to realize that God is doing for us what we could not do for ourselves.

[Permission to use the Twelve Promises of Alcoholics Anonymous for adaptation is granted by A.A. World Services, Inc.]

To the Newcomer

Welcome to Families Anonymous. We know how you're hurting, because we too were once new in this fellowship. We were confused and in pain, but we found hope in our FA meetings.

We can't tell you what to do. We can only share our experiences with you and tell you how we found the strength to deal with our problems. Some of us have loved ones who are recovering from addictive disease. Others of us have loved ones who choose not to recover, at least for the present.

We've learned that we can live fuller, richer lives by studying and practicing the Twelve Steps of Families Anonymous. The despair that brought us to this program no longer dominates our lives. We have learned that we have rights and deserve to be happy, but it's up to us to create that happiness.

These changes did not come about overnight. They happened because we attended our FA meetings, found sponsors, studied the Steps, made phone calls to other members, and turned to a Power greater than ourselves.

You are no longer alone. Welcome to Families Anonymous.

TODAY I WILL open myself to another so that both of us can be helped.

January 2

Hope

When I attended my first Families Anonymous meeting, I met people with the same problems I had. They were going through experiences just like my own. They seemed to know exactly what was going on in my home.

The immediate relief of finding people I could identify with was astonishing. Their stories were similar to mine, and they were cheerful, helpful, supportive, and encouraging. I felt my first ray of hope: Surely I, too, could learn to cope.

The FA program promised that I could find better ways to deal with life even though someone close to me was an addict. I listened to everyone and made a commitment to *keep coming back*.

I felt such a great relief! I had found people who cared and *understood*!

TODAY I WILL find encouragement in other people's progress and share my own experience with newcomers searching for solutions.

Step One

We admitted we were powerless over drugs and other people's lives–that our lives had become unmanageable.

It is difficult to accept Step One. Although some newcomers can accept the concept of being powerless, most need time to reach this realization. When I came into the program, I thought being powerless to control my loved one's life made me a failure. Because of my pride, I attempted to force others to behave at a level of maturity where responsibility, integrity, and truth had real meaning.

I did not understand then the power and control that drugs and alcohol have over a dependent user. Before I followed the Twelve Steps, I tried to purge my chemically dependent family member of his destructive thoughts and actions—but to no avail. When I finally accepted the fact that he, and he alone, could change his own behavior, I began to understand Step One.

TODAY I WILL accept my lack of power while maintaining my freedom to change the things I can. "I can change myself—others I can only love."

January 4

Serenity

When I find myself in mental and emotional turmoil because of my anxieties and fears, I have the ability to put those thoughts "on hold" and shift from negative to positive thinking.

Instead of feeding my anxieties, I can foster a sense of wonder and gratitude. I can notice a beautiful sunset, watch children as they laugh and play, marvel at a bird's flight, or smell the fresh countryside after a summer rain. What beauty and serenity can be found just by observing!

When I am quiet and still, I can be in touch with my Higher Power. Knowing my God is there, I allow my fear to be replaced by faith.

TODAY I WILL work to replace anxiety and fear with gratitude and serenity.

One Day at a Time

One day at a time. Families Anonymous members repeat this slogan frequently because it helps them reach some sense of peace and stability during times of chaos and pain. How could I possibly learn to live that way, after a lifetime of planning and managing other people's lives, months and even years in advance?

Yet little by little, out of sheer desperation, I have begun to live one day at a time. And, to my surprise, it works. This day-at-a-time philosophy guides me calmly through the troubled waters of life with rebellious teenagers and the frictions that are part of marriage. It keeps the little daily irritations in life just that—little.

The calming slogan of *One day at a time* is one of the most important tools we have for building a better life.

TODAY I WILL think only about this day, without worries about tomorrow or regrets for yesterday.

January 6

Worry

Worry is a habit acquired through repetition. My legitimate concern for someone who's misusing drugs can reinforce the worry habit until it becomes a powerful, destructive obsession.

I am learning that I can change worry and negative thoughts through conscious, deliberate practice. I *can* replace worry with positive ways of thinking. I *can* cultivate good habits through repetition, just as I once cultivated bad ones.

Worry is not productive. It does not solve problems. I need to let go of those people and situations that cause me to worry, and I need to turn them over to the care of my Higher Power, entrusting Him with the outcome.

Only then can I replace these obsessive thoughts with grateful thanks that a Power greater than myself is taking care of my concerns better than I ever could.

TODAY I WILL refuse to worry, knowing my worrying has never helped my Higher Power get the job done.

Detachment

I tend to think of my children as extensions of myself. If they are successful, so am I. If they fail, I fail as well. Although this isn't true, it takes a lot of Twelve Step study and self-education to detach myself from this idea.

In Families Anonymous meetings, I hear a reassuring statement—that the only way young people grow into responsible, happy adults is by being allowed to accept the consequences of their own actions. They don't profit from nagging and preaching, which only make them feel more worthless. Nor do they benefit by being protected from the natural outcomes of their choices.

As parents, we know quite well that none of us is perfect. Our children often learn to use our feelings of guilt and inadequacy to manipulate us. This is not healthy for parents or children. Without FA, I could not have learned to resist such manipulation. In the program, I came to see that my suffering is not terminal. By relying on a Higher Power and making both successful and unsuccessful attempts to detach from my children's problems, I have grown stronger, and my children have learned to stand on their own feet.

TODAY I WILL allow others the dignity of learning from their own mistakes and the privilege of choosing their own paths.

January 8
Humility

As I continue in Families Anonymous, I realize that if I am to progress, I have to "prepare the soil." The greatest obstacles to progress are my own character defects: false pride, impatience, intolerance, unrealistic expectations, unreasonable anger, and a need to control others.

What a mountain of defects to confront! But I can begin by countering pride with humility. In this program, humility does not mean self-abasement, or groveling. Humility, as FA sees it, means taking a good look at myself and finding that I am neither all-powerful nor all-knowing. It means seeing myself as I really am, with full recognition of my good qualities as well as my faults.

When I make an honest appraisal of myself, I achieve a new dimension of self-awareness. Playing down or denying my good qualities would be dishonest, so I gratefully acknowledge these assets as gifts from God and try to use them in my life.

TODAY I WILL guard against pride and arrogance and seek to grow in true humility.

How Important Is It?

Slogans are some of the best tools of our Families Anonymous program. Short, pithy reminders of the essentials keep us on track and out of trouble, provided we use them. With steady use, the slogans become dependable internal "tapes" that can reconfigure and rebalance our thinking when we slip back into old, unproductive ways.

How important is it? is one of my favorite slogans. How important is it for me to offer my opinion at all? How important for me to take someone else's inventory? How important to be right, listened to, or obeyed? All of these questions remind me when I am straying from the straight path of recovery, getting bogged down in detours and dead ends.

How important is it? got me through my son's determination to wear earrings and jeans with holes in them. *How important is it?* reminded me that my daughter's friends do not have to be my friends. *How important is it?* prodded me to get myself to an FA meeting when I was sinking into apathy and depression.

We in FA know what is important for our recovery: going to meetings, working the Steps, keeping in touch by phone, and doing things that lend to our own health and well-being, regardless of what others may do.

TODAY I WILL focus on what's important and let the rest go.

January 10

Acceptance

Acceptance is not easy. It means that I must look at a situation with honesty and with the realization that sometimes I cannot change it, cure it, or control it. It just is as it is. When I am deeply hurt, I may react with anger or rejection. Disappointment makes it difficult for me to accept the painful reality or the chemical dependency of someone I care about.

Fear also makes acceptance difficult. I want to rescue instead of letting that person learn the painful lessons of mistakes. I feel helpless, watching as he treads the thin line between rebellion and independence. He rejects my advice, and the consequences are grim.

The Twelve Steps help me realize and accept the fact that I have no power or authority over another human being. Acceptance means acknowledging that I cannot eliminate chemical dependency, any more than I can make a sick person well.

TODAY I WILL invite acceptance to put an end to futile struggles and set me free to grow.

Living in Fear

As I deal with the person close to me who misuses drugs, my reactions take many forms. Anxiety, fear, worry, and obsession are the chief ones. When I let my imagination run wild, it creates ever-new fears to replace the old ones. The short-lived relief when something I dreaded doesn't happen is all too often replaced by still more fears.

This is the insanity we speak of in regard to the family disease of addiction—allowing absorption with the situation to become an obsession that drains all our energy for appreciating the gifts of life *today*.

I must consider alternatives or face serious consequences. My life is at stake. How long can I survive in the grip of such damaging fear? After all, I have accomplished nothing with my constant worry about what might happen tomorrow. When I calm down enough to examine my fears, I see that most of them concern the future.

When I project a future that may never happen, I am only borrowing trouble. Living one day at a time is the only way to have a life.

TODAY I WILL name my fear and let it go, and I will look for the gifts of this one day.

January 12

Step Two

Came to believe that a power greater than ourselves could restore us to sanity.

My first reaction to this Step was indignation. I came to the Families Anonymous program to change my *child's* behavior, and now this Step tells me that *I* am insane.

I steamed about this Step for quite a while. It was only with the help of others in my group that I finally came to see that if *I* wasn't insane, some of my actions certainly were. Through the patience of my FA friends, I came to realize that I had gone to insane lengths to try to *change* the behavior of my drug-using child, refusing to admit that I lacked the power or ability to do so.

Gradually, I came to believe I could be restored to sanity if I listened with an open mind and delayed judgment on those ideas that had sounded too radical at first. With the help of a Power greater than myself, I *could* change my outlook. And at that point my own healing would begin.

TODAY I WILL cease relying on my own power and begin trusting in a greater Power.

To Be or What To Be?

The Families Anonymous reading titled *Helping* says, "My role as helper is not to *do* things for the person I am trying to help, but to *be* things…."

At first I wondered what I should *be*. Over time, as I continued to participate in FA meetings, I learned the value of being…

- responsible for my *own* feelings
- strong enough to stand up for my rights
- loving enough to allow others to be what they choose to be
- aware of the realities in my life
- rational in a crisis
- consistent in my FA program, to the best of my ability
- diligent in my study of the Twelve Steps

I know that living this way will bring me serenity. As a fringe benefit, my example may also inspire those I would like to help.

TODAY I WILL be the best *ME* that I can be.

January 14

TLC

To most people, TLC means "tender loving care." In Families Anonymous, TLC can mean "*tough loving care*." If I really love someone in a healthy way, I will refuse to let that someone manipulate me. I will no longer allow another person to be the hub of my universe or the focus of my own happiness in life.

TLC means that I stop participating in the games played by someone who misuses alcohol or other drugs. I stop covering up his mistakes and refuse to make excuses for his behavior. I may even have to say, "I love you, but I can only live with a person who is clean, sober, and responsible. I love you, but I will not bail you out of jail. I love you, but I will not pay fines or attorney's fees to get you out of trouble."

TODAY I WILL practice the kind of tough loving care that nourishes the growth of myself and others.

Energy Conservation

Families Anonymous is an energy-conservation program. As soon as I began to apply the Serenity Prayer and the Twelve Steps to my everyday life, I stopped wasting energy. No longer do I fret over what I see as the wrong actions of others. I need not waste my breath on long lectures. I don't have to protect others from the consequences of their own mistakes. Best of all, I can cease doing things for my loved one in an effort to change him.

I find now that I have time for myself: time to take up a new hobby or renew an old one, read a book, enjoy music, go shopping, work out, plant a garden, play tennis, or putter around the workshop. I have the energy and clear mind I need to do my own work and enrich my life.

TODAY I WILL use my energy for living my own life more fully.

January 16

A Higher Power

Being in Families Anonymous a few months revealed to me that for many years I had tried to be my loved one's Higher Power. But things went badly. Obviously I was not qualified for the job!

Then somewhere I heard the prayer, "God, make me a channel of your love, and let me know when I get in the way."

Hearing that, I could see myself casting a huge shadow over my son's life. By shielding him, I was blocking out a Higher Power he could understand. I needed to step aside and let my loved one see for himself.

The FA program gave me the strength to stop fixing, rescuing, instructing, sheltering, and all the other enabling actions I always did as a parent. I was soon rewarded with the opportunity to see a boy become a man. And in the process I became a person in my own right.

TODAY I WILL have faith in my Higher Power, myself, and those I love.

Detachment

A word we frequently hear at Families Anonymous meetings is "detachment." One might imagine that detaching means giving up all love for the chemically dependent person. But this is far from the truth.

Once we detach ourselves from involvement in the *illness* of drug or alcohol abuse, we can freely love the person who has the illness. We do not stop caring; we simply detach emotionally from the user's *problems*. We can pull away and refuse to get tangled up in the consequences of chemical abuse. We let our loved ones feel the painful results of the drugs. We allow them to accept responsibility for their own actions. We stop protecting them. For it is pain that lets a sick person know that he or she needs treatment, and it is pain that often leads to healing and recovery.

TODAY I WILL remember that I help the most when I help the least.

January 18

To Believe or Not To Believe?

Do I constantly watch and wait to catch my addicted loved one using drugs, or do I turn a blind eye to those things I'd rather not see? Do I pry into her personal effects, hunting for proof, or do I ignore the obvious? Do I believe everything she tells me, or do I refuse to believe a word she says? Which attitude leaves me with greater self-respect?

Whether using or abstaining, the addict needs my trust, compassion, and understanding. Above all, she needs the dignity to make choices and to experience the consequences of her decisions. When her choices are damaging, she will grow by learning from her mistakes. When they are wise, she will experience many rewards.

If I must face up to something unpleasant, I will try to do so honestly, then let it go. Until then, my own life will be more serene if I have faith and detach instead of searching for the lie.

TODAY I WILL choose to believe the best of others, in so far as circumstances will allow.

Power

Families Anonymous taught me there are two ways of looking at Step One. It is true that I am powerless over someone else's life. On the other hand, it is equally true that everyone else is powerless over *mine*.

For a time, the drug user in my life had complete control of our home and happiness. His actions left me feeling nervous, sleepless, angry, and afraid. I was reacting to unpleasant situations in ways I didn't like, and he capitalized on my weakness.

Families Anonymous helped me understand that others have such power over me only if I *give* it to them.

I keep coming to meetings to learn, step by step, how to regain control of my own life and stop giving away that control to others, no matter how much I love them.

TODAY I WILL claim my power to bring about my own serenity.

January 20

Keep it Simple

Our Families Anonymous slogans are life-savers for new members of the program. When we are floundering in the heavy seas of the family disease of addiction, anything that helps us stay afloat seems like a miracle. The slogans provide that buoyancy.

Keep it simple was the one I used most in the early stages of my recovery. Keep what simple? Everything!

I want to keep things as simple, direct, and clean as possible, because my life has become confused, cluttered, and chaotic. I have lost sight of what matters and what doesn't. I can't remember what is my responsibility and what belongs to someone else.

Keeping it simple helps me to begin clearing up the confusion. Keeping it simple means going to meetings regularly and doing the Step that's appropriate at this stage of my recovery, without trying to do all twelve at once. It means reading some short piece of recovery literature daily. It means keeping my sleep sufficient, my exercise regular, my diet healthy, and my communications clear.

When that old, familiar mass of confused, chaotic, compulsive thought starts to surge up in my mind, I remind myself to *Keep it simple* and let go of everything that doesn't matter at this second, this minute, this hour, and this day.

TODAY I WILL keep everything as simple as I can.

Listen and Learn

I go to Families Anonymous meetings because there I find people who are going through problems just like mine. I go to find out how they can smile and have hope in spite of unsolved problems. If I listen, I can learn how the Twelve Steps have helped others and how they can benefit me.

It feels good to go to FA meetings and express my negative thoughts and feelings. But unless I replace my negative attitudes with better ones, they'll only creep back into my consciousness.

It's important to share at meetings, but it's equally important to *listen*. If I do all the talking at meetings, I'll miss many ideas that may give me new insights. And I cannot give my attention to what others say if I am consumed with my own thoughts.

TODAY I WILL listen and learn, allowing new ideas to enter my awareness.

January 22

Living Today

Why do I let my thoughts go racing off into the future? Why do I persist in imagining so many dreaded things that may or may not occur? Panic and worry have never helped me solve next week's or next year's problems today.

When I waste time imagining all these "maybes" and "what ifs," I become so overwrought that I am incapable of dealing with *today*. On the other hand, if I focus on this day or this hour and use it to the best of my ability, I will have no time left over for projecting a future that may never come. A wise man once said, "Sufficient unto the day is the evil thereof."

Finally, it helps me to remember that every day need not be a struggle or a duty. There are gifts in each new day: kindness, patience, generosity, beauty, love. When I let go of the future and the past, I am ready to live most fully this one precious day, with all its gifts.

TODAY I WILL refuse to spoil today with worry about tomorrow.

Step Three

Made a decision to turn our will and our lives over to the care of God as we understood Him.

In Step Three, each Families Anonymous member has complete freedom to develop a relationship with a Higher Power according to his or her own feelings and beliefs. When I make my personal decision to turn to this Higher Power, I can then let go of the problems I cannot solve, the questions I cannot answer. The change is not easy for me, because until now I have always tried to manage my own world.

Surrendering the reins of control to an unseen Power seems unfamiliar and, at times, downright uncomfortable for me. Turning it all over does not mean I sit back and do nothing. I will still need to ask for guidance and then take action—or be wise enough *not* to act at certain times. I can do the footwork, but the results are truly beyond my control. The sooner I realize this, the sooner I will find serenity.

TODAY I WILL give up my willful strivings and let my Higher Power show me the way.

January 24

Willing to Grow

When I first became involved with Families Anonymous, I attended meetings with nothing more than my physical presence. For a while, I waited for the magic answer. I desperately wanted to know how to change my drug user into something he was not—and perhaps never could be.

But I persevered, attended more meetings, and began to learn an important truth: By focusing my energy inward, I *could* change my situation by changing *myself.*

Through faithful attendance at my FA meetings, I continue to discover new ways to change myself. Here I can express my feelings honestly with others who give me honesty in return. If I am sincere about my program, I can bring order back into my life.

My focus sharpens. Changes begin within me. My meeting becomes a means of establishing a spiritual backbone. I know I am getting better.

TODAY I WILL look for at least one way to grow.

The Fourth Destructive Force

When I dwell on the hurtful actions of the addict in my life, I give him power over me. I allow the drug user to hurt me over and over again when I keep remembering and retelling every detail of his behavior.

Newcomers to the fellowship of Families Anonymous need a chance to unload all the refuse that's been cluttering up their lives, but they are not helped when they continue to dwell on it week after week. The FA program is one of growth and recovery, of facing up to things honestly and then *letting them go*.

Horror stories told in Families Anonymous meetings do very little to help anyone. It's better to use meeting time for sharing ways we have found to make our own lives better. This helps us more than blow-by-blow descriptions of a drug user's behavior.

I go to FA meetings to learn ways to change the things I can change. I can make my own life fuller and richer by turning my attention to thoughts and activities that make me feel good. Each day offers some gift, if I will seek it out.

TODAY I WILL let go of the past and focus on enriching my own life.

January 26

Blame

How easy it is to blame others for all my misfortunes! Families Anonymous and the Twelve Steps teach me to resist this easy way out and to correct what I can. In recovery, I stop blaming the schools, my youngster's friends, or our changing society. Blaming gives me a constant excuse for not taking action. Instead, I express my anger and frustration and then look for what I can change.

There are some actions I *can* take. Instead of blaming others for the negatives in my life, I can focus on the positives: health, sunshine, interesting work, a good book, a funny incident.

I am responsible only for my own actions. I needn't offer excuses for the behavior or actions of others. Nor will I allow others to blame me for their mistakes.

TODAY I WILL take responsibility for my own actions and feelings and no one else's.

Giving

When I first came to Families Anonymous, I experienced understanding, compassion, and caring. I was given hope. Passing this hope on to others has become a very important part of my new life.

FA provides me with an opportunity to give to others while allowing me to see my *own* problems in a new light. The more I give of myself, especially in sharing with the newcomer, the more chances I will have to grow.

I often find solutions to my problems by taking the time to listen to a fellow member's difficulties and helping that member deal with them. Both of us learn, and my serenity deepens.

Giving to someone else in a healthy way helps me feel better about my recovery and my program. Giving myself to my Higher Power releases me from unnecessary worry.

TODAY I WILL be ready to give to others and to myself.

January 28

Step Four

Made a searching and fearless moral inventory of ourselves.

At first, the Fourth Step looked impossible. I wanted to avoid checking over my past, fearful that the negatives would outweigh the positives. I didn't want to admit all my weaknesses or even list my good points.

Other Families Anonymous members sensed my feelings and asked me to tell something positive about myself. The purpose of the Fourth Step, they said, is to arrive at a *realistic* self-portrait. My friends in FA lovingly helped me to see that everyone has strengths as well as weaknesses.

By owning my strong points, eventually I became able to accept my faults too. I soon came to realize that these defects of character were the cause of my unhappiness. As long as I refused to acknowledge them, I could not grow. I needed to take Step Four to get the full benefit of this program.

TODAY I WILL rejoice in my character strengths and search out those faults that still stand in my way.

Guilt

"Where did I go wrong?"

How many times I asked myself that question during the worst days of my loved one's addictive illness! Old habits of placing blame often left me blaming myself for everything that went wrong.

In Families Anonymous, I found reassurance that I had done the best I could under the circumstances. I discovered that I did not *cause* my abuser's illness, I could not *control* it, and I cannot *cure* it.

When I laid down this load of guilt, I was free to think more clearly. I learned new ways to deal with my own problems and allow others to work out theirs.

TODAY I WILL be good to myself and stop carrying the burden of guilt.

January 30

Meditation

When I take time to listen for the guidance of a Higher Power, I can find peace. Only then can I understand the Families Anonymous message in the Twelve Steps. From this quiet understanding, I gain the courage and wisdom to deal effectively with the one whose problems brought me to FA.

What extra concerns, duties, and unnecessary activities can I trim out of my days in order to remove myself from the intrusions of modern life? Do I turn off the radio and television and look for a quiet place? Do I ever turn off my internal chatter and allow myself to hear what my Higher Power would have me know? If I answer yes, I may find a better way to live.

TODAY I WILL make time to be still and listen.

Let Go and Let God

Trying to cope with someone who misuses alcohol or other drugs or is verbally or physically abusive can cause such mental chaos that I may feel there is no help for me. In spite of my ceaseless efforts to solve all my problems, things seem to go from bad to worse. My best efforts are useless. I feel helpless and hopeless. I don't know where to turn or what to do.

When I am at my lowest point, face to face with my inability to manage or control, that is the moment I can acknowledge my need of a Power greater than myself. One of the greatest tools Families Anonymous has given me is the reminder, *Let go and let God.* My Higher Power can help me with the things I cannot change or control if I truly let go and honestly admit that I am powerless over other people.

At times of crisis, when decisions have to be made and I am too distraught to think clearly, I need all the more to draw on the strength of my Higher Power and the experiences of other FA members. I cannot do it alone, but with the support of others who care, I can do what I need to do.

TODAY I WILL let go and let God, using the tools my FA program gives me.

February 1

Self-Esteem

As my recovery progresses, I realize that I must take the focus off everyone else and put it back on myself. For a time I lost my sense of identity and my self-esteem. I felt I had failed as a parent, as a spouse, and in all my other relationships. I finally came to grips with the fact that I needed to change my own life in order to be a whole and effective person once again.

The first step in this process was to change my negative thinking to positive. The encouragement and support I found in Families Anonymous, the readings, the sharing, and a sponsor's loving concern convinced me that no one can destroy my self-esteem without my permission. My self-esteem does not depend on what others think of me. Rather, it depends on what *I* think of *myself* and what my relationship is with my Higher Power.

TODAY I WILL treasure my self-esteem, refusing to let anyone else's opinion diminish me.

Addiction—A Disease

When some people come to Families Anonymous for the first time, they have trouble accepting the fact that addiction to mind-altering substances is a disease. All they can think of is the horrible way the addicted person has been treating family and friends.

It is difficult for family members to recognize disease when all they have seen is hostility, contempt, lies, cheating, and even stealing.

But all this is part of addiction—the disease that causes its victims to choose drugs over people. Until we accept addiction as a disease, we remain stuck at the level of hostility and contempt. We feel the need for revenge. We want to punish the addict for what he or she has done to us.

As I work the FA program and begin facing and dealing with my resentments, I start seeing how they damage my peace of mind, my spirituality, and the well-being of my family relationships. I will be far better off when I react to my addicted family member without punishment or negativity. Then I will be free to grow.

TODAY I WILL accept addiction as a disease and lay aside my feelings of hostility.

February 3

Choices

Attending Families Anonymous meetings has opened new avenues of thought for me. I've learned I have choices! My life does not have to be unmanageable. Some situations I can change; others I can't, but I can at least change my attitude toward them.

This thinking, alien to me at first, was soon very welcome. Instead of persisting in my unsuccessful attempts to change another person whose behavior causes problems, I have learned to approach these problems with a new perspective. Those horrible scenes of the past do not have to be repeated over and over in the present. I do not have to cover up, condone, or accept another person's irrational and destructive behavior. By working my own Twelve Step program, I have no time left to try controlling someone else's life.

My new attitudes and perspectives have lessened tensions and brought my first ray of hope that things can improve. New thinking has broken up my patterns of despair and defeat. I can *choose* to be serene!

TODAY I WILL look for the helpful choice in any situation that presents itself.

Anonymity

One of the nicest things about attending Families Anonymous meetings is being comfortable enough to share thoughts, problems, and ideas without fear of gossip or ridicule. Anonymity protects my family and me from false tales and idle conversation.

Untold harm can result if those who attend FA meetings fail to be impressed by the importance of this tradition of our fellowship. I have a sacred responsibility to others in FA never to reveal their secrets or repeat their stories. Our tradition of anonymity demands that I separate problems from the people who bring them out into the open.

Remaining anonymous is also a tool for helping me succeed in the FA program. When members or guests attending our meetings are free of any identification by title, position, profession, social standing, or community status, I can be honest about my feelings and just be myself.

TODAY I WILL keep in mind the Twelfth Tradition: *Anonymity is the spiritual foundation of all our traditions, ever reminding us to place principles above personalities.*

February 5

Letting Go

Letting go has always been a great struggle for most of us. It involves much more than simply releasing our loved ones to their Higher Power.

By sharing, working the Steps, and being faithful to our readings in Families Anonymous, we are helped to let go of a misguided sense of responsibility. The fellowship encourages us to let go of attempts to control, influence, or shape the destinies of others. We learn to relinquish false pride, senseless argument, and caustic criticism. We leave behind the horror of the past, detaching ourselves from regrets, remorse, guilt– all the old fruitless ways.

Letting these things go is a vital step in our recovery. Doing so allows us to fear less, love more, and enjoy each day more fully. As we let go, we begin to listen, to learn, and to support instead of trying to direct and control.

TODAY I WILL cherish this day alone and *let go* of days past or days yet to come.

Gratitude

Sometimes my life seems a shambles. What's the use? Why go on? This is a time to sit down and think about gratitude. I ask myself, "What do I have to be grateful for?" A beautiful sunrise? Health? An interesting career? Books in the library? My Families Anonymous group?

We are surrounded by opportunities to educate ourselves, to create a small thing of beauty such as an arrangement of autumn leaves, or to collect smiles in the grocery store.

By gratefully focusing my attention on the work at hand and the wonderful people in my life, I get on with the business of living and leave the problems I cannot solve in the hands of my Higher Power.

TODAY I WILL remember to be grateful.

February 7

Taking Inventory

Making a searching and fearless moral inventory of myself is an important part of the Families Anonymous program.

Facing my faults may be harder than acknowledging my assets. Doing so is often very painful, but I have gradually learned that unless I name and claim my faults, I can never overcome them. I am discovering that, with humility, I can admit my faults without feeling worthless and shamed. Humility restores my vision, without crippling me emotionally or spiritually.

Experience teaches me that the greater the pain, the greater the opportunity for personal growth. While I cannot achieve perfection, I can at least search out and seek to correct my own imperfections, with my Higher Power's help.

TODAY I WILL continue my honest appraisal of myself.

Step Five

Admitted to God, to ourselves, and to another human being the exact nature of our wrongs.

An essential ingredient of the Fifth Step is admitting the *real* me to God, to myself, and to another human being in the hope of gaining serenity.

I make all kinds of excuses for staying locked inside myself. After all, I have an image to protect. Opening myself up threatens my sense of privacy and independence. Making myself vulnerable feels like losing control.

But I forget that often my best access to my Higher Power is through other people. Unity comes through community. Surprisingly, sharing my past with another person lessens the sting of deeds I once thought were unforgivable.

TODAY I WILL risk seeking and finding my Higher Power through honesty with other people.

February 9

Feelings

"You shouldn't feel that way!" We may remember being told this when we were children, or even just last week. At times we even tell *ourselves* we shouldn't feel as we do.

But my feelings are real. They don't go away when I "stuff" them or run away from them. They burrow deep inside and make me sick, unless I find a way to express them and work through them.

In Families Anonymous, I've learned to express my feelings honestly, in meetings or through phone calls to fellow members. And I have also begun to express my feelings to members of my immediate family.

At the same time, the FA program teaches me to allow others to take responsibility for *their* own feelings.

TODAY I WILL make it my responsibility to own my feelings.

A Family Disease

Chemical dependency is a family illness. When one member has the disease, the whole family suffers.

The same story was told two thousand years ago in the Biblical parable of the Prodigal Son. When the down-and-out boy returned home, shamed and guilty, his self-esteem was at its lowest point. Yet when he asked for his father's forgiveness, the father forgave him at once, in spite of his own private suffering. The elder son resented the attention showered on his wayward brother and refused to have anything to do with the celebration.

This family was a long way from being fully healed, but the process was underway because two members took the first steps: admitting the problem and sharing each other's pain.

When even one person in a family changes a negative attitude, others respond. I'm glad the story doesn't tell what happened to the elder son. Instead, he will always symbolize the choice each of us faces daily: to cling to our misery and continue to hurt, or to confess our pain and reach out for loving acceptance wherever it can be found.

TODAY I WILL share my pain and find loving acceptance in Families Anonymous regardless of whether anyone else in my family seeks help.

February 11

Serenity

I am no longer powerless when I find myself agitated and in mental turmoil, because I can rely on my Families Anonymous program to get me through the pain. I *can* make a positive choice to break the vicious cycle. I *can* take a deep breath and allow myself time to slow down. I *can* choose to be calm and at peace.

I *can* be gentle with myself and quietly get in touch with my inner feelings, knowing that my serenity comes from within. I *can* ask my Higher Power to be with me.

Despite all my unsolved problems, I *can* open my heart to serenity, one moment and one day at a time.

TODAY I WILL find serenity in my own growth in recovery.

Step Six

Were entirely ready to have God remove all these defects of character.

When it was time to begin Step Six, I thought how easy this would be compared with the previous Steps. How wrong I was!

Identifying my defects had taken all of the honesty and dedication I could muster. How surprised I was now to discover that I was definitely not ready. I had found it difficult enough on Step Five to share my defects with God and another human being; now Step Six said that I must go even further.

The thought of having my shortcomings removed really scared me. After all, they were comfortable and familiar, even if they were wrong. If I released them all, would anything be left of the real me?

Eventually I saw the absurdity of this thinking, even while clinging to it, and realized I did not have to work this Step all at one time. I could choose to give up just one or two defects and still experience growth. I would have many tomorrows to give up the rest.

TODAY I WILL give up whatever character defect I can, knowing that if I wait until I can give them all up at once, I may never start.

February 13

Love or Power

In *The Infernal Grove* by Malcolm Muggeridge, the author refers to an inscription said to have been found on an ancient North African stone:

"I, the Captain of a legion of Rome, serving in the desert of Libya, have learnt and pondered this truth: There are in life but two things, Love and Power, and no one has both."

Is this true? I suspect it is. As much as we may wish for power over the lives of others, particularly the lives of our children, we long even more for love. And if we can have just one or the other, who among us would give up love?

Admitting our powerlessness over others may not be so hard when we know that doing so opens us to the creative power that runs the universe. That power is love.

TODAY I WILL choose love over power and be thankful for my choice.

Love

Love—that's the theme of Valentine's Day. Love is wonderful! All of us want and need love.

But there are all kinds of immature love: the "magical" kind by which young people envision finding the perfect mate and living happily ever after, the smothering kind that does too much for others, the self-punishing kind that forsakes one's own needs in favor of another person's selfish demands.

The best love is a mature love, a healing love that recognizes and speaks the truth in humility and hope. Our Families Anonymous program is based on "tough love"—love grounded in reality which undertakes its actions in self-responsibility.

Real love means admitting one's mistakes and making amends wherever possible. It means looking at life with a clear eye, without self-pity, accepting what is and changing what we can. It means living day by day in gratitude for God's love for us—the greatest love of all.

Love sometimes gives and sometimes asks to receive. Love bestows self-acceptance and self-esteem. Love challenges and consoles. Love laughs and cries. Long ago, a man named Paul turned from his wrathful ways and reorganized his life around three things: faith, hope, and love. And the greatest of these, he discovered, was love.

TODAY I WILL love others appropriately and love myself as well.

February 15

Step Seven

Humbly asked God to remove our shortcomings.

Step Seven, for me, was a natural conclusion to the three preceding Steps. I made my inventory and shared it. I reached the decision to have God remove my defects, and now it was time for action.

The very fact that I had to pray to a Higher Power once again was humbling. In so doing, I was admitting to myself that there was indeed a force greater than I.

I really wanted to be free of all the warped thinking on which I had based my earlier decisions. I wanted to start afresh, to become a new *me*, with new insight, new knowledge, and new ways to handle problems. Never mind my reservations! I would give myself some time to get accustomed to this changed situation.

I prayed, and afterward I really felt less alone than I had before. True, I still had to do my part, but now I could do it believing that if I was ready to give up my shortcomings, my Higher Power was ready to remove them.

TODAY I WILL meet my Higher Power halfway whenever I want help.

Say What You Mean

In the Families Anonymous program, we learn to stop making idle threats and to project only those consequences we are prepared to carry out.

One member sat down with his son, who would soon be 18, and said, "I love you very much and always will, but you are doing things you can't get away with indefinitely. I love you, and I'm concerned about you, but I will not spend even ten cents on lawyers' fees or bail to get you out of jail. And if you are arrested on drug charges, I probably won't visit you in jail."

The day came when this father had to keep his word. It meant nine days of holding his peace, not interfering, and wondering if this was the right course. He found strength by calling other FA members, who reflected his feelings and shared his concern.

Much later, his son, who by then was on the road to recovery, said, "I found out my folks had finally blown my cover. I hated them, but I also realized it was up to me to decide what to do with the rest of my life."

TODAY I WILL remember that threats are ineffectual, but natural consequences can create change.

February 17

Meetings

"How long do I have to keep going to these meetings?" In reality, there is no "have to" in the program of Families Anonymous. There are only choices.

But some of us have answered this question: "Until you *want* to go." At first we go to meetings to find out how to cure or help our loved ones. Then we find out we can work only on our own recovery. Seeing the progress others make is a powerful motivation for us too.

As we work the Twelve Steps, we grow stronger and begin to feel better. We keep coming back. Eventually we find ourselves looking forward to meetings. We hope our friends will be there too, so we can gain fresh new insights, knowledge, and growth. We also hope to find some newcomers there, so that we can share with them what we have gained in FA.

TODAY I WILL work to keep my Families Anonymous group strong, so that there will always be a meeting to renew my strength and hope.

Expectations

Expectations can get us into trouble. If we are inclined to expect the worst, we may become sick with worry or paralyzed with fear.

Unrealistic expectations lead to disappointment: for example, expecting a particular result when we leave "helpful" literature where someone else will read it. Expecting total recovery from an addict who's been clean and sober for three weeks, three months, or three years can also set us up for a devastating plunge. Expecting too much from ourselves will often lead to grief; no one is perfect.

Perhaps the only safe expectation is that a Higher Power will bring about a correct solution, now or later, and that the answer to our prayers will be *Yes, No,* or *Wait.*

TODAY I WILL be open to the future rather than trying to create it through my expectations.

February 19

From Pain to Gain

Everyone in Families Anonymous has known a lot of painful feelings: anxiety, fear, resentment, anger, hurt, grief. Such emotions are a natural part of being human, although we often wish we didn't have to experience them.

With time, I have learned to not shy away from emotional pain, because I realize that the pain signals a need for some kind of change in my life—an attitude, a reaction, a different choice. When I am hurting emotionally, something in my life is out of balance. Am I clinging to self-pity, continuing to focus on the other person's problem, or hanging back from some new behavior that will enrich my life? "No pain, no gain," our recovering friends tell us.

Pain invites me, first of all to acknowledge and accept it, then to seek its origins, and then to take what prayerful action I can to restore balance to my life.

It is in passing through the fire that the metal of our lives is purified and made strong. I will accept my emotional pain as an invitation to wholeness. I will make it an asset instead of a liability.

TODAY I WILL try to discern the purpose in any pain I encounter. It may be an opportunity to grow.

Communications

Have you ever noticed how often control-addicts begin a sentence with the word *why*? I had no idea it was a form of criticism, control, or butting in when I prefaced my communications with this word. But the person to whom a "why" remark is addressed is immediately put on the defensive. She must justify why she did or did not, will or will not do as I think she should. Generally, "why" provokes another argument, and things get blown out of proportion.

Mature individuals usually welcome positive suggestions; they are capable of accepting or rejecting them without feeling nagged or put down. Not everyone is so mature, however. Most of us in dysfunctional families have fragile self-esteem, and in our communications, "why" is better left unsaid.

Asking "why" is often an unnecessary backward look at something painful. Perhaps a more useful question for our purposes is, "What now?" Instead of interrogating another about his or her intent, motives, or impulses, it's better to take a calm and realistic look at what our next move should be.

TODAY I WILL focus on, "What now?" instead of the critical, "Why?"

February 21

Using the Slogans

When I am confused and don't know which way to turn, a slogan may be the only thing that puts me back on track.

Slogans are short, easy to remember, and come straight to the point. During my early days in Families Anonymous, I memorized several of them: *Keep it simple. Let go and let God. Easy does it. One day at a time.* Later, when a crisis or a problem arose, it was like having money in the bank. One of those helpful slogans floated up unfailingly from the depths of memory and carried me through.

Early in the FA program, I wondered whether I could ever keep it all straight. My head was spinning with Steps, Traditions, responsibilities, needs, feelings, and wants. I could have become totally bewildered by this multitude of things to do "right," if I hadn't started with the slogans.

The first one I learned was *Keep it simple.* What does it mean? To me it means reduce a problem to the simplest terms, find the simplest action to take, say the simplest word.

Let go and let God followed that one, and then the others: *Easy does it. One day at a time.* Slogans that really help.

TODAY I WILL learn or use at least one slogan to help me stay serene.

Powerlessness

Time and time again, a newcomer at a Families Anonymous meeting will ask, "Isn't it my duty and responsibility to control my teenager?" On the surface this idea might seem to make sense. The truth is, however, that we can offer only guidance, not control. And communicating *any* information to one whose mind and body are affected by chemicals may be impossible anyway.

As caring people, we find it difficult to accept the sad fact that an addicted youngster cannot respond to a family's normal rules and regulations. How helpless we feel in admitting that lectures, scoldings, or punishment have little or no effect on a sick, drug-dominated personality.

It takes more than a few FA meetings to understand the full truth of Step One of the program: *We admitted we were powerless over drugs and other people's lives....* We in the program can patiently and lovingly share our own experiences of how we learned to accept the hard but healing reality of Step One.

TODAY I WILL reach out to a newcomer who is still struggling with Step One.

February 23

Listening

A common pitfall in listening is the temptation to start mentally preparing our own response, to be sure our "words of wisdom" will be properly heard and understood. When we do that, we are really only half listening, getting ready to convey our opinions. This is closely related to domineering and controlling. The people with whom we're talking can't fail to notice our less-than-total receptivity. That's when communication starts to break down.

Webster's definitions of *listen* are "(1) to pay attention to, to give ear, hear, tune in; (2) to hear with thoughtful attention, heed; (3) to be alert to catch an unexpected sound."

If we want others to listen when we speak, we must learn to listen when *they* speak. This is important in a one-on-one conversation and essential for constructive group meetings. We can learn much more when we truly listen. It is then that many answers are revealed.

Real communication is a two-way system. Failing to listen can be overcome through hard work; the payoff is definitely worthwhile.

TODAY I WILL remember that God gave me *two* ears and only one mouth.

Recovery

We came to our first Families Anonymous meeting full of fear, guilt, suspicion, hurt, and hostility. We came seeking ready solutions and instant cures for another's problems. What we found at FA were other people who had grave problems but had nevertheless managed to find sanity and even serenity.

Listening well, we learned that a change had to occur within ourselves, and that patience and working the program could be the catalysts for eventual recovery.

We learned to deal with our fears and to forgive ourselves. We acknowledged our hurts and accepted comfort. We gave up suspicion and hostility in favor of letting go and trusting in a Higher Power. This change allowed us to accept the small successes of daily living and to avoid the pitfalls of projecting into tomorrow. Our greatest gains have been serenity and a lasting, ever-expanding recovery.

TODAY I WILL live out of the knowledge that recovery begins with me.

February 25

Release With Love

My sister has found a Twelve Step program to help her stay clean and sober. Happy for her, I now wonder how I should behave where she's concerned. Fortunately, through Families Anonymous, I am learning to release with love.

Sobriety is wonderful for my sister as well as for those of us who care about her. But FA has taught me that her sobriety is more likely to endure if she chooses it strictly for her own reasons. She will not be inclined to "stay clean" for anyone else.

Similarly, I've learned that I cannot pin my hopes and happiness on her sobriety. I love her, but I set her free to work her own program, just as I am free to continue my own program and growth.

Thus I release my sister from the need to stay clean to please me. If she stops drinking alcohol or using other drugs merely for my sake, she will not be clean or sober. She will just be "not using."

TODAY I WILL release my loved one to her recovery and get on with living my own life with joy.

Resentment

Often at a Families Anonymous meeting, a newcomer tells a story filled with pain and resentment. Overwhelmed with bitterness, the person wants to hurt and destroy those who have caused the family to suffer so much.

At one time, nearly all of us have felt this way, but today we've grown to understand more about resentments than we ever thought possible.

We know that harbored resentments only create more resentments. If we allow them to grow, there is little room in our minds and hearts for anything else. Holding on to resentments harms us more than it does the person we continue to resent. The only way we can save ourselves is to make a conscious decision to abandon our resentments before they destroy us.

Some people write their resentments out on paper, then burn the paper. Some people tell them to a sponsor or confess them to a trusted friend. Some people compose brief affirmations about letting go of the person they resent; then they repeat those affirmations until they become free.

TODAY I WILL release my resentments in order to make room for gratitude in my heart.

February 27

Tomorrow

My projections of what tomorrow might bring used to fill me with so much fear that I was unable to concentrate on anything or anyone else.

Then I heard the slogan, *Just for today.* Relying on this slogan day by day took many of my worries and fears away and gave me time to appreciate where I am *now.*

Through the Families Anonymous program, I am learning that it's no good worrying about what tomorrow may bring. I can enjoy today and let tomorrow take care of itself.

No longer need I spend valuable time and energy dreading those frightening tomorrows. For, after all, each tomorrow is merely one more precious *today.*

TODAY I WILL live the journey of self-discovery, one day at a time.

Self-Respect

I feel foolish now when I think of all the things I once did to cover up, "so others would not know." Now I accept the fact that my addicted child is sick. As I accept this reality, the damaged love between us can begin to heal. I can walk by him today, touch his shoulder, and say, "I love you"—something I would have thought impossible a few years ago.

I want to give him his independence. I know that his self-respect suffers when he depends on me. My own self-respect would be damaged if I allowed others to do everything for me. I would miss the good feeling that comes from tackling a challenge and seeing it through. Now I respect my son's struggle to grow, and he respects the progress I have made.

TODAY I WILL maintain my self-respect and allow others to claim their own.

February 29

Images

Before my addicted daughter committed her energies to getting well, I found it almost impossible to be in the same room with her. Her appearance, speech, behavior, and lack of consideration for others irritated me beyond belief.

Finally a wise friend said, "Try painting a mental picture of your daughter with S-I-C-K in big red letters across her forehead." It worked! Whenever her behavior had me climbing the walls, I traced those imaginary letters and was able to feel compassion for her.

Then she decided to get well. She accepted the offer of treatment, worked her program, and went faithfully to meetings. Yet she still reverted to old behaviors at times. I tried to paint that imaginary word, S-I-C-K, again, but it no longer worked. After that, whenever her behavior bothered me, I painted a new mental picture of my daughter—radiantly recovering and living in her own image of wellness.

TODAY I WILL accept what is and imagine the very best that can be.

Step Eight

Made a list of all persons we had harmed, and became willing to make amends to them all.

At first, some of us thought Step Eight might be a more appropriate task for the ones who had brought us to Families Anonymous. Wasn't it *they* who had made a mess of our lives?

After working Steps Four, Five, Six, and Seven, however, we realized we had harmed more than a few people ourselves. Perhaps we had focused on the drug user to the detriment of others in the family. Our distress might have made us neglect our obligations to a spouse, an employer, or a friend.

I came to see that I had harmed myself most of all. At the height of this family illness, I became a "ghost" of my former self. I let go of those things that make my life worth living, and I let my appearance get frayed and ugly. I even lost my sense of humor! I had a lot of amends to make—to myself as well as to others. It would be a big job.

The second part of this Step says, "…became willing…." Until I could say that I was truly willing to tackle it, I had to humbly ask for help in facing Steps Eight and Nine.

TODAY I WILL become willing to make amends.

March 2

Words Change Lives

In order to change my negatives to positives, I work on my vocabulary. I make a conscious effort to eliminate *global* words like *always, never,* and *forever* and to replace them with *sometimes* and *often*.

Should is another word worth replacing. My motto is, "I will not *should* on myself or others." In place of *should,* I can say *could, may,* or *might.* These words are open-ended and imply a *choice*.

A favorite word I've added to my vocabulary is *invite*. I cannot force another person to take an action I desire. I can only invite him or her to do so. Still, when I issue an invitation, I'm prepared to allow a person to accept or reject it.

My new vocabulary makes me better equipped to make connections with people and to be nonjudgmental. I'm finding that words really do change lives.

TODAY I WILL modulate my voice, choose my words thoughtfully, and temper them with kindness.

Resentment

Before coming to Families Anonymous, I had an endless list of people I thought were destroying my son's life. I blamed his friends, the school, drug dealers, the recording industry—you name it, I blamed it. My resentments kept me in a constant turmoil, always wanting to even the score.

I also harbored many resentments because I kept trying to help people who didn't want to be helped and thus showed no appreciation for what I did. Then there was the type of person who played helpless, almost begging for assistance, only to resent my efforts when I did step in. My whole life seemed like an open wound.

Today I know, through my Twelve Step program, that nothing has the power to hurt me *unless I allow it*. I do not have to be dependent on others for my contentment. With the help of a Higher Power, I have the choice of replacing my resentments with thoughts of love and gratitude.

Now when I start to find fault with "them," I find serenity in writing a list of things for which I am grateful.

TODAY I WILL cancel resentments with an attitude of gratitude.

March 4

Sponsors

Let's hear a cheer for the unsung hero in our midst—the Families Anonymous sponsor!

A sponsor is someone a new member chooses as a guide to the FA way of thinking and living. One's choice of a sponsor is made on the basis of empathy, trust, and mutual agreement. Being asked to be a sponsor is an honor, and the responsibility should not be taken lightly.

Why have a sponsor? Most of us come into the program confused and hurt. Our lives have been torn apart. Our emotions are in turmoil.

At first I was so shattered, I was even afraid to speak out in meetings. But I chose someone for my sponsor, and having that person to call on at any hour was a true blessing. No one else was there when things went crazy. No one else had the patience to listen for what must have seemed hours; to tell me, cheerfully, the same thing again and again; and to lead me through the Twelve Steps of FA.

My sponsor is someone in whom I can confide, someone who can show me my hidden faults and love me anyway. How can I thank my sponsor? The best way is by being a sponsor for someone else.

TODAY I WILL consider getting or being a sponsor in my FA group.

A Better Way to Live

At a recent meeting, I was shocked to hear a woman say she was grateful for her child's disease. I assumed her troubles had unhinged her mind! But she went on to explain that she had found a better way of life in Families Anonymous and was happier now than she had ever been.

Not all of us can take such a philosophic view, but we can follow her logic. Her child's addiction introduced her to the Twelve Steps. If we faithfully live the Twelve Steps, we can have a better life.

How pleasant it is to rid ourselves of all that excess baggage we've been carrying around! No more hypocrisy, no more false pride (or its nasty counterpart, false humility), no more controlling or soul-destroying anger.

I can throw away my fears and trust in a Higher Power instead. I can get rid of the guilt, make my amends, and be honest. Maybe I'll even surrender my impatience, resentment, and sarcasm as I grow in this new life.

No one ever said it would be easy, but constant vigilance and total commitment to my FA program may lead me to the day that I too can thank God for this trial.

TODAY I WILL enjoy the gifts of the FA program and its better way to live.

March 6

Step Nine

Made direct amends to such people whenever possible, except when to do so would injure them or others.

As I see it, the purpose of making amends is twofold. First, I want to convey to the persons I have harmed my wish for things to be right with them. I don't want to repeat the wrongs of the past. Second, I need to know that I have honestly done all in my power to right my wrongs, and that I no longer have to carry a load of guilt for past deeds.

The second part of this Step suggests there are some people to whom I can never make amends. However, I *can* write a letter of apology and then destroy it. In addition to that, I can change or *amend* my behavior toward those who might be injured by an open apology.

TODAY I WILL look for the right time and place to make amends.

Forgive and Forget

Our Families Anonymous program gives us a chance for personal renewal, beginning with honest self-evaluation when we take the Fourth Step. Here is an opportunity to look at our actions, both right and wrong. We see the actions and reactions that caused us sorrow, hurt, and guilt. In Step Five we let them go.

When we go on to Step Nine and make amends to those we have harmed, we make proper restitution. We hope to be forgiven for wrongful actions of the past. Asking forgiveness teaches us how to forgive in return.

In the case of loved ones—those who have behavioral problems, addictions, or both—we must forgive and work at forgetting the heartache of former times and focus on what is positive and hopeful today. We must let go of the pain of sleepless nights, the chaos and confusion, the violence and the terror.

Can all of this be forgotten? Perhaps not entirely, but forgiven it must be. Until we can forgive and forget, we can at least *let go of it*. The basis for these changes is our FA program.

TODAY I WILL wipe clean the slate of the past, letting nothing stand in the way of my recovery.

March 8
Walls

Once there was a man who grew up in an alcoholic home. He learned at a very early age how to build a wall of security around himself, a barrier against the pain and insanity all about him. He grew up, married, and had a lovely family, but only his wife showed affection toward the children. He loved his family, but he couldn't show it.

When his teenage daughter became chemically dependent, he appeared to take it very well. He kept a stiff upper lip and stuffed all those "bad" feelings away, deep down inside. He never let his anger, fear, or pain come out.

One night at a Families Anonymous meeting, however, he saw a father break down and weep for his lost child, and something broke within his own heart. When he reached out to his fellow sufferer, his own tears—to his surprise—began to fall. Telling of his own hurt in an effort to comfort another, he found comfort for himself.

He could finally express his own painful feelings. He could let out the pain. And when he did so, he found he was not alone. Waves of love came flowing back to him from the group. His invisible wall crumbled, and he began to heal.

TODAY I WILL push away the walls around the pain that I need to share in order to let it go.

Detachment

A favorite Families Anonymous topic is *detachment.* We discuss it endlessly, praise it constantly, and have more trouble with it than almost anything else.

We all love our children, even those who are still misusing drugs, but none of us want to be hooked into the emotional highs and lows that drugs can create. We all want to turn over our problems to our Higher Power, yet we keep grabbing them back. Detaching makes good sense, but it's terribly hard to put into practice.

Sometimes a simple ritual helps us make the breakthrough. At a recent meeting, the group was surprised to find a helium-filled balloon tied to the back of every chair. Attached to each balloon were a pen and a label.

The leader explained, "Write on the label the name of the loved one from whom you wish to detach. Stick the label on the balloon. Then bring the balloon and follow me outside." The whole group silently walked outdoors and, at a given signal, released their balloons and, symbolically, their loved ones to God. Some held on longer than others; some watched until the balloons were only specks in the distance. Many couldn't see the balloons for the tears in their eyes. Letting go with love is never easy.

TODAY I WILL adopt whatever method will help me to let go.

March 10

Passing It On

When I had to enlist the aid of the court in regard to my child, I was scared. I had no idea how to proceed. I feared the consequences and worried about the effect on my child. Was this the right thing to do? How would I implement such a procedure? Where would I go?

I had a lot of outside information, but it was the honest and courageous sharing of experience in my Families Anonymous group that helped me make up my mind. Some of my fellow members had faced the same choice, known the same anxieties. They spoke openly of their experiences, pointing out my options, calming my fears. Knowing the pros and cons helped me to make a good decision.

How helpful it is to realize that I am not alone! Many people have gone through the same ordeals as I and are willing to share their sorrows and joys. When a newcomer arrives, weighed down by mountains of trouble, I remember all the help and love I've received and do my best to pass it on.

TODAY I WILL hand the program on, making yet another link in the FA chain of sharing and love.

Doing My Best

I had my own qualifications for being a caring parent long before I joined Families Anonymous. I was always home for my children. I baked cookies and joined the PTA. I drove my offspring everywhere, took part in school activities, and volunteered for playground duty—even when it snowed. I kept a "perfect" house, was a "perfect" mother. Yet I had less-than-perfect children.

How could this happen? I'd made all the "right" moves, had done all the "right" things. How could it be? I felt very hurt and, yes, resentful when my child became ill. Through no fault of his own or mine, he had the disease of alcoholism.

I realize now that there was nothing I could have done to change things. When I hear a mother berate herself because she had a job outside the home or might not have paid enough attention to her children, I can reassure her. My drive for perfection made no difference at all.

Chemical dependency is a disease, and whether we are stay-at-home mothers or career women, whether we are easy-going or strict—none of these factors makes one iota of difference. My serenity depends upon accepting this reality.

TODAY I WILL give myself credit for doing my best with the knowledge and skills I possess at the time.

March 12

Traditions

When we first come into Families Anonymous, the Traditions seem relatively unimportant. Our minds are filled with our own troubles. It's hard enough to understand the Twelve Steps and a few basic concepts, let alone think about group unity and public relations.

Once we become comfortable with the program and start to recover, however, we begin to see the necessity of the Traditions. For most of us, the group is our lifeline to sanity. Where would we be without our group? Who else would listen and understand? Where would we find the support we need for difficult decisions or even just a friendly smile and a hug? Without our groups we would surely be out there again riding that emotional roller coaster day after day.

Just as we personally need the Steps, our *groups* need the Traditions. The Traditions guide us, keep us on an even keel, set limits, and define our purpose. When we follow the Traditions, no one dominates a group. The Traditions provide unity within the group and with all other FA groups.

TODAY I WILL respect the Traditions and see where they contain a lesson for me.

Helping

When my addicted sister is in the midst of a crisis and I rely on my Families Anonymous program, some friends and family members who are unfamiliar with FA accuse me of being cruel and cold, of abandoning my sister. I begin to feel my old guilt returning as they press me to help my sister get out of her self-inflicted difficulties.

This is the time when I most need to call an FA friend for strength. I need someone to remind me that the best help for my sister is often to do nothing, even though well-meaning but misguided friends and relatives outside the program may define that as no help.

Families Anonymous reminds me that the best help is *discipline by consequence*, an approach that allows my sister the dignity of learning from her mistakes.

TODAY I WILL gladly rely on FA for help as I allow others to help themselves.

March 14

Bonuses

Families Anonymous has given me many things of value: a better way to live, freedom to follow my own interests, time to be good to myself, and a good measure of serenity.

And working the FA program has brought me an unexpected bonus in the form of better relationships with my friends and co-workers. No longer do I give unwanted advice or try to take charge. I allow others the dignity of their own choices, and I'm a better listener when I do not judge. I accept frustration more calmly and refuse to waste energy fretting about matters over which I have no control, such as late buses and unavoidable disappointments.

Best of all, I'm more giving and receiving of affection, and I can relish others' successes without envying them.

TODAY I WILL look for new bonuses in living the Twelve Step way.

Listening

When I first came to Families Anonymous, I was consumed with the hopeless mess of my situation. For several meetings, I was so focused on recounting my drug-dependent child's transgressions that I couldn't hear what others had to say. I didn't grasp what the program was all about.

After my third meeting, a kind woman gave me her phone number. "You have a big burden to lay down," she said. "Call me and we'll talk."

The next day, I did as she asked. She was a good listener. Finally, I stopped talking. "Thank goodness you're done with that," she said. "Your job now is to keep coming to meetings and listen to what others have done in similar situations."

I was puzzled. Why didn't she tell me how to cure my son's addiction?

At the next meeting she sat beside me, and when I started on my tale of woe again, she put her hand on my shoulder. "Every time you tell it, you allow him to hurt you once again." I finally heard what she was trying to tell me. I stopped talking, started listening, and began to grow.

TODAY I WILL listen for the lesson that's right for me.

March 16

Who Am I to Judge?

I've always thought myself a good judge of character. What's more, I used to make it my mission in life to help others mend their ways, make better choices, and improve their lives. I even offered God a few valuable suggestions!

But when I came to the program of Families Anonymous and committed myself to the Twelve Steps, humility worked its way into my thinking. I realized I do not have all the answers. My children must make their own responses to life. I cannot do it for them. And I cannot imagine the kind of world my grandchildren will inhabit, so how can I know what's best for them? I don't even know for certain what's best for *me*, other than cultivating my own serenity.

It's been hard for me to get over a lifelong habit of judging others, but FA has helped me begin to let it go.

TODAY I WILL judge no one, not even myself.

Step Ten

Continued to take personal inventory and when we were wrong, promptly admitted it.

Before living the Twelve Steps, I made it my habit to conceal unpleasant feelings and evade discouraging realities.

The Tenth Step is a reassuring reminder that never again do I have to live more than one day at a time. The painful past has finally been put to rest.

But the Tenth Step is also a humbling reminder that there is no final stage of perfection. A slip backwards to old negative patterns is always a possibility, and I need to be on guard every day against egocentricity and false pride. Step Ten helps me follow the "beacon" of Families Anonymous.

TODAY I WILL live in the freedom and serenity that comes from honesty, humility, and self-acceptance.

March 18

Comparisons

My neighbor's daughter is a doctor; another friend's son is in law school. But I'm not bragging about my own two children, for at this time they appear to me to be choosing to waste their lives.

Many of us in Families Anonymous foolishly cloak ourselves in shame because our family members do not excel. We allow ourselves to feel like parental failures because our children are not fulfilling the images we projected when they were infants. How silly we are to think this way! How self-important to believe that everything depends on us!

Our children make their own choices. Most of us did the best parenting we could with all the knowledge and skill we possessed. All we can do now is stand back, love our children, give them room to grow, and then live our own lives fully.

TODAY I WILL be happy for anyone's success, refusing to assume blame or make comparisons.

Joy

When things are going well for me, I sometimes cannot enjoy my good fortune. "This can't last," I tell myself and hold back my joy. "I might get my hopes too high, and then the crash will hurt even more."

Such an attitude is bound to be the result of years of building emotional defenses, and it will take hard work to replace it with an attitude of greater freedom. But I know that my hesitation in rejoicing *can* be unlearned. The Families Anonymous Twelve Step program is helping me learn how to do it.

Study of FA literature has helped me to take one day at a time and to live in *this moment* and savor it. When I do that, I recognize that I am living in grace, and I can enjoy it and be grateful.

TODAY I WILL release my fears and accept the joy in my life.

March 20

Hands Off

Even though the person I've been concerned about for so long is clean and sober and working on her own recovery program, sometimes I still "walk on eggs," fearful that I may say or do the wrong thing and cause her to use again. I'm tempted to give her articles and "helpful" literature, believing she needs this kind of support.

Fortunately, my Families Anonymous sponsor reminds me that the power to make my daughter get well or stay sick does not rest with me. "Cultivate your own serenity," she says. "Your daughter has her own program, a sponsor to guide her, and plenty of literature to study. All you need to do is love her."

I'm thankful to have someone who sees through my efforts to "help" and recognizes them for what they are—subtle attempts to keep my hand on the tiller and control another person's life.

Gratefully, I turn my attention to my own life, look for new adventures, or polish up a few aspects of my recovery that I've overlooked or neglected.

TODAY I WILL follow my own program and leave my loved one to interpret and practice her own.

Service

We are asked to perform service for Families Anonymous. We are even told that service helps us recover from the family illness that keeps our homes in turmoil. "How will my setting up the chairs and preparing coffee make my situation any better?" I wondered. Reluctantly, I took on the job of treasurer and ordered literature from the World Service Office.

Before long, I was well acquainted with all of the FA publications and had learned a lot about the program. Later, I took on the job of group secretary for a period of six months. These responsibilities drew me back to meetings and kept me growing in the program. My home life even improved as a result of the service I undertook for the group.

Without the help of those who are willing to serve, there would be no FA, and I would still be floundering around in the confusion that was my daily portion before I found the program.

TODAY I WILL do my part to keep Families Anonymous alive and well, so that others who need this program can recover too.

March 22

Whose Recovery?

When my son found his own Twelve Step self-help group and became clean and sober, I was overjoyed. But then I got away from my own program and started thinking, "What if...?" and "This can't last." My serenity suffered.

Even though he was very happy in that first six weeks of sobriety, he *did* eventually relapse; and for several years thereafter, he was in and out of recovery.

In spite of my son's shaky situation, Families Anonymous helped *me* stay off the roller coaster of emotional ups and downs by detaching myself from his actions and concentrating on my own program. When fear crept into my consciousness again, I was ready with positive affirmations: "He's extremely happy when he's clean; he knows where he can go to gain sobriety; his sober periods are getting longer and longer; he *will* make it *if he chooses recovery.*"

TODAY I WILL focus on my serenity and allow others to find their own.

Work Your Own Program

Work your own program. This was the most helpful suggestion I heard at my first Families Anonymous meeting. I wasn't sure *why* I needed to do this, but all through the following week I kept this thought in mind. Every time I started to tell someone what to do, I would ask myself, "Is this any of my business? Is that my responsibility?"

In a household with my spouse and three teenagers, I usually found the answer to be, "No." So I tried to work my program, and mine alone. It wasn't always comfortable. I was sure my way was better, and things didn't get done as quickly as I would have liked. I bit my tongue and turned to my own tasks anyway.

By the end of the week, I felt pretty good. I was under far less pressure, and I even found some free time for myself.

Working my own program is a basic part of life for me today. I no longer waste time wondering what someone else is doing or saying. If I'm supposed to know, I'll hear soon enough. If something appears to need changing, I consider what may need changing in me.

Now *Work your own program* is my main message to newcomers in Families Anonymous.

TODAY I WILL allow others to work their programs while I take care of my own.

March 24

A Full Pitcher

We learn in Families Anonymous that addiction to alcohol and other drugs is a family illness. This illness often causes us to lose some of our best attributes, such as humor, imagination, and creativity.

When I realize I've become filled to the brim with resentment, bitterness, sarcasm, self-pity, and despair, I put my creative imagination to work. Visualizing myself as a pitcher, I mentally pour myself out, emptying myself completely of every drop of negativity, discouragement, and despair. When they are all gone, I then sit quietly for a bit and fill myself again—this time with faith, forgiveness, honesty, gratitude, patience, humor, and praise.

Once I have recharged myself with these fresh new thoughts, I can then imagine I am a *cool pitcher* filled from a well of serenity. Other thirsty FA members can "drink" from this same well, so they too can be refreshed.

TODAY I WILL live in the joy that comes from thinking life-giving thoughts.

The Power of Love

I have often tried to play the role of Higher Power. When I look back on my attempts, I realize how futile they were.

A Higher Power can direct, decree, demand, and judge. These are the parts of the role I usually try to play. But the Higher Power of my understanding can also show kindness, mercy, compassion, and love. And these are the attributes I am prone to overlook.

How often in the past I searched for the impossible and tried to assume a power that was not mine to possess! I set up expectations for my family and roles for my children, trying to make them clones or mirror images of myself. I created difficulties for myself and others when my hopes and dreams fell victim to reality.

My poor fantasies and unrealistic expectations can never equal the beauty and power of the true creation that surrounds us all. I can use what little power I possess to create confusion, crisis, disappointment, self-defeat, chaos, and discontent. Or I can use my power to create acceptance, harmony, loving detachment, encouragement, and peace. This is the power I wish to claim.

TODAY I WILL create possibilities by exercising my power to love.

March 26

Acceptance

One of the hardest things for me in the Families Anonymous program has been learning to let go and accept the fact that the outcome is not mine to control.

As I grow in my ability to let go, however, things do get better. I now accept the reality that my drug-dependent son suffers from a disease. I accept the fact that his behavior is often unacceptable. Even though the choices he makes are his, and his alone, I don't have to like them or approve of the way he lives his life.

Through acceptance, I become able to live *my* own life and involve myself in fulfilling activities without thinking of what my son might be doing with his life. I do this, recognizing all the while that what he makes of his life is up to him, so long as none of my rights get trampled on.

Acceptance has allowed me to change: from fretting and being constantly on edge to feeling free in my mind; from walking on eggs to standing firm; and from crying to caring, even amid unsolved problems.

TODAY I WILL accept what is, stand up for myself, and work for what may yet be.

Anger

Before coming to Families Anonymous, I automatically assumed another person's anger was directed at me. Now I realize that my drug-dependent children's anger usually has little to do with me and is often just their way of avoiding responsibility for their own actions. And often it's their own self-hatred being projected outward onto someone or something else.

As I see my own self-confidence and inner strength grow through working the FA program, I no longer allow myself to be hurt by my children's anger or anyone else's. I am able to remain calmer and more objective even in the face of other people's rage.

TODAY I WILL claim my own serenity in spite of someone else's anger.

March 28

What FA Has Done For Me

Families Anonymous has let me know that I am not the only person in the world with family frustrations. With the support of others in my FA group, I've learned to maintain positive attitudes in the midst of these frustrations.

FA has helped me stop thinking of myself as a failure. The program reminds me that any failures are in the past. I know today that I can make the best of the present situation and build on it. FA has led me to accept myself first, which then helps me to be more accepting of others. Once I have done that, I can make further steps toward recovery.

FA shows me that anger is a normal human emotion, one that I can express and use constructively. I don't allow it to dominate me.

FA reminds me that I cannot control my child. The program gives me the opportunity to stand aside, let him make his own decisions, and learn to live with the consequences.

TODAY I WILL give thanks for all FA has taught me.

Releasing With Love

Thank you, Families Anonymous, for helping me reclaim my sanity. Before FA, I stared out the windows during the wee hours, paced the floors, and shed gallons of tears. Now I sleep nights and seldom find anything to cry about other than a very sad movie!

Working my program and sharing experience, strength, and hope with other FA members have given me the ability to release my child with love. I no longer try to change him. I am letting him be himself—whatever that may be. And trusting my life to a Higher Power has made the whole world seem new.

I am truly a happier person. Thank you again, Families Anonymous, for showing me a better way.

TODAY I WILL surrender others and myself to the grace of a Higher Power.

March 30

Step Eleven

Sought through prayer and meditation to improve our conscious contact with God as we understood Him, praying only for knowledge of His will for us and the power to carry that out.

When my life first began to crumble along with my hopes and dreams, I cried, argued, and became depressed. I tried to control, to change people, to talk sense to my addict, but I did not pray.

I needed God, so I started trying to pray. But after I found Families Anonymous and reached the point of preparing for Step Eleven, I discovered I'd been praying for control over people and events. I had been treating God as an errand boy who was supposed to carry out my orders. I was talking but never listening.

True prayer and meditation call for honest sharing of pain and hopes, reflection on all that I have learned about my role in the larger scheme of things, trust in a Higher Power, and a willingness to listen and wait.

I was grateful when I could allow Step Eleven to help me grow in patience, understanding, and wisdom.

TODAY I WILL seek a quiet place and time to improve my conscious contact with God.

Reach Out

Before my first Families Anonymous meeting, I lived in a constant state of panic. Two of my children were destroying themselves with alcohol and other drugs. I was desperate to find a way to help them.

The FA fellowship helped me realize that in order to be of help to them, I must *first* be willing to be helped myself. With the readings, meetings, and the Twelve Steps to rely on, I started learning to do this *one day at a time.*

Eventually my panic was replaced by the realization that I could not handle this crisis alone. I asked my Higher Power to give me the wisdom I desperately needed. With God's guidance, I found the answers I sought through my FA "family." They supplied the necessary love, encouragement, and support.

Now I keep coming back, even during my calm periods, for I want to share with others what was freely given to me.

TODAY I WILL reach out to an FA friend.

April 1

Changing

I was convinced that everything would be fine if my daughter gave up her destructive behavior. Well, she did give it up. And guess what? Life did not turn into a garden of roses. She changed, but I didn't. She had a program and began getting well, while I continued my own obsessive efforts to manage her life, even though she was 37 years old.

Finally she let go of me and told me there was a program for people like me if I wanted to feel better. After "all I'd done for her," I felt deserted.

But I did eventually go to Families Anonymous. At first it seemed as though I had found a whole group of people who needed my help! I was probably the first person that anyone ever wanted to kick out of FA. Fortunately, my group was very patient with me. Weeks and months went by, until I finally settled down to get to know myself. What a pain I was! I certainly would not have picked me for a friend or even an acquaintance.

It takes courage to change, but I'm finding it exciting. And I intend to keep changing for the better, because I have a lifetime in which to live and grow.

TODAY I WILL find the courage to change and be patient with myself as I do.

Laughter

There was no humor in my life before I began attending Families Anonymous meetings. Devastated by crises and wrapped up in my own pain, I could find nothing to laugh at.

I remember my first FA meeting and feeling horrified that people were having a good time. Why, some members actually laughed out loud! At the time, it seemed to me like laughing at a funeral.

Before the meeting ended, I realized they had a bond. I found that honest sharing of similar experiences brings a different perspective. My burdens didn't seem so heavy after I shared them, and I gained insight from hearing how others had handled much worse situations. At the end of that evening, I was even smiling myself.

The humor I found at FA helped me overcome my fear of being there. Humor initiated a change in my attitude, offered hope, and kept me coming back for more. Now when things get bogged down again, I remember that first meeting—and I can smile.

TODAY I WILL take nothing too seriously, cherishing the healing power of laughter.

April 3

It Works for Me

When my son entered a treatment program, I learned that chemical dependency is a disease. In the aftercare program, I learned about Families Anonymous. I felt a strong need for support in my own recovery, so I decided to give FA a try.

What a blessing! Others in the group had similar problems. I no longer felt alone. My FA group supplied caring friends and a safe place to share both problems and progress with others who understood.

Today I work on my own recovery, even though my son has not yet achieved sobriety. He continues to use drugs, and this creates many stressful situations. Without the support of FA, I wouldn't be coping with this situation at all.

I have learned how vitally important it is for me to work my program, take care of myself, and turn my son and myself over to our Higher Power. No matter what I say or do, I cannot control another person.

TODAY I WILL cherish my own progress in recovery, regardless of the choices others make.

Live and Let Live

Of the many valuable ideas I've gained from Families Anonymous, the slogan *live and let live* remains one of the most meaningful for me. It helps me keep my attention focused on living my own life as well as I can while I allow my daughter the same privilege.

When I catch myself wanting to do for her what she can do for herself, I work to change my approach by remembering to *live and let live.*

The same slogan has brought a bonus into another area of my life: it is helping me outgrow my tendency to judge and criticize others. When I concentrate on living *my* life as fully as I can, I am too busy for such nonproductive attitudes.

When I remember to *live and let live*, I grow in tolerance and respect for people whose attitudes and behavior differ from my own.

TODAY I WILL live a full life while letting others do the same.

April 5

Anger

When I attended Families Anonymous for the first time, I had just placed my 15-year-old daughter in a hospital for treatment of chemical dependency. I was consumed with anger and frustration over her drug use. "How could she do this to herself and her family? And what's wrong with us? Why couldn't we fix this problem ourselves?"

As I began to understand her illness and its destructive effects on me, my anger was soon replaced by a rekindled love for my daughter and a personal commitment to do what I could to help both of us recover.

The principles of FA have helped me change the only one I can change—myself. Whatever my daughter's situation, I'm learning to release her to her Higher Power with love.

TODAY I WILL continue to apply the principles of FA as I replace my anger with understanding.

First FA Lesson

The first time I attended Families Anonymous, a father explained to me that my daughter's addiction was a medically recognized disease, a condition one might compare with diabetes, in that it is incurable but can be arrested through appropriate treatment. He also told me that her addiction was not my fault.

Both of these ideas were new to me. They gave me a welcome feeling of relief and the beginnings of new insight into our situation.

At first I went to FA to help my daughter, but after a few meetings I kept on attending to help myself. FA is helping me understand myself, my daughter, and our circumstances in a realistic and constructive way. We have come a long way from that first meeting, and I will always be grateful to all the people in the program who provided the principles so vital to my personal growth and serenity.

TODAY I WILL be grateful for the progress I've made.

April 7

Step Twelve

Having had a spiritual awakening as a result of these Steps, we tried to carry this message to others and to practice these principles in all our affairs.

We have a responsibility to pass on the gift of Families Anonymous. We need to do this for others, and for our own benefit too. We pass on this gift in order to grow.

There are many ways we can carry this message to others who need the FA program: through faith-based fellowships and other organizations; through doctors, counselors, and treatment centers; and through sharing with those we meet in our day-to-day lives. We must always be ready to help other people who are in trouble. We can give them information about FA, offer hope, and tell how the program helps us recover.

But we must be tactful in our approach. We take care to simply offer people the FA tools—and then step back and allow them to use these tools if and how they choose. Our role is not to teach, but to show people where they can go to learn and to find help. And if others see serenity in us, perhaps they will want it for themselves.

TODAY I WILL carry the FA message as well as I can. I don't need to be perfect to do this, only willing and sincere.

Happiness

A young couple came to their first Families Anonymous meeting filled with anger and fear. Their lives had been turned upside down, and the pain seemed almost unbearable. They could hardly wait for the meeting to start, so anxious were they to share their pain and anguish with other suffering parents.

But they were in for a shock! They had expected moaning and groaning, rage and fury, yet they found themselves surrounded by laughing and smiling people who radiated peace and joy. Had they come into the wrong room? Were all these people crazy?

Not any more! These people were recovering. They had found a basic truth and were living it: "My happiness does not depend on anyone else."

The new couple was bewildered by the absence of what seemed to them an appropriate degree of misery, but they kept coming back. Soon, they too began to smile and laugh a little. They found that peace of mind was no longer dependent upon what their drug-using child did or did not do. Their serenity was their own responsibility and too precious to give up to others.

TODAY I WILL be responsible for creating my own happiness.

April 9

Needing People

There's a line in a song that goes, "People who need people are the luckiest people in the world." I'm one of those lucky people. I'll be the first to admit that I do need people. I need the people of Families Anonymous.

When I found FA, my heart was broken in a million pieces, and I didn't know how to put it back together. I still don't have every single piece in place, but at least my heart is mending and still beating.

The wonderful healing fellowship of FA has given me brothers and sisters to whom I can relate, for we are all one with the same problem.

TODAY I WILL open my heart to another person as a way to help myself heal.

One Day at a Time

One day at a time. "Oh, there's another one of those slogans. They sound all right at meetings, but putting them into practice is another thing."

That's how I felt the first time I attended a Families Anonymous group. But little by little, I came to see that this particular slogan teaches me to be good to myself today, let go of the unhappy times of the past, and avoid worrying about tomorrow. It invites me to fill today with as many pleasant experiences as I can and to help others do the same.

Living one day at a time is especially necessary for those of us who know the pain and confusion of the family disease called chemical dependency. It's all too easy for us to project problems into the future that may never materialize. Fortunately, we have our friends in FA to help us remember to live *one day at a time.*

TODAY I WILL make this one day a celebration of life.

April 11

Self-Pity

One member of our Families Anonymous group told us that she was so crushed and defeated by her child's drug addiction that she walked everywhere with her head down and her eyes cast low, so that no one could see her hurt and despair. By doing so, she kept her field of vision extremely limited—cracked sidewalks, bird droppings, mud puddles, and dirty shoes.

When she found Families Anonymous and stepped out on the Twelve Step road to recovery, she raised her head to see the break in the clouds with sunlight shining through, the birds darting from tree to tree, a rainbow after a shower.

Had she continued to wallow in self-pity, her eyes would have remained closed to the beauty in each day. If we dwell on the hurts and miseries of yesterday and dread the possible pain of tomorrow, we miss out completely on today.

TODAY I WILL broaden my outlook, appreciating the gifts this new day brings.

Self

"Self" is a powerful word. Attached to other words, it carries either a negative or a positive message. Like so many other intangibles, its impact depends upon the way we use it.

When we come into the Families Anonymous program, our "selves" are usually negative ones: self-doubt, self-recrimination, self-pity, self-justification, self-blame. At times, we behave in ways that are self-centered, self-serving, self-defeating, and just plain selfish. We do not recognize that we are self-imprisoned in our denial and unwillingness to change.

But as we work the Twelve Steps, we discover some other "selves": self-awareness, self-respect, self-control, self-confidence, self-esteem. "I can change myself," our FA reading tells us. As we grow and change, we discover the lovable, worthy selves that have been there all along.

If we continue reaching for the positive "selves" that are ours to claim, we eventually arrive at the best "self" of all: selflessness. When we get to that point, nothing pleases our new self more than sharing the program with someone who needs it. As we discover who we are, we let go of negativism and self-centered ways.

TODAY I WILL become the best self I can be.

April 13

Lessons

I had to learn to accept many things when I started coming to Families Anonymous. The first thing was powerlessness. Surely I couldn't be powerless over my own son! After all, hadn't I managed to control him all these years? Well, if I had, what a mess I'd made of it!

Now that I have turned over all that control to my Higher Power, things certainly are working better. It's funny how much we can learn in FA when we get honest with ourselves. And being honest with myself was the second thing I learned in FA.

How often I had tried to justify my faults. I always had such good reasons for what I said or did! Somehow the truth stands out when we read the FA material over and over.

TODAY I WILL acknowledge the many lessons my FA program has taught me.

Control

Oh, how I tried to control everyone in my life! But all I ended up with was frustration and anger. Why couldn't my family see that I knew what was best for everyone?

Thank God I found the Families Anonymous program, for it showed me how to release my loved ones from the tyranny of my nagging ways. Through the FA program, I learned to gain a measure of control over myself—the only person I am capable of controlling. What a feeling of freedom came when I gave up trying to manipulate everybody else's life and concentrated on doing something positive about my own!

When I find myself starting to take over again, I remember who is *really* in charge of my family and me, and I give back to my Higher Power the control I had thought was mine.

TODAY I WILL ask my Higher Power to remove any urge I may have to control other people or situations.

April 15

Roles

I kept saying to myself, "My daughter is the one with the problems. She's the addict who causes all the upheaval in our family." That was before I found Families Anonymous.

As I became better informed about addiction, I learned that this disease gets better only when the addict wants it to get better, regardless of how much the family may long for changes.

Coming to meetings and faithfully reading FA literature, I learned that each member of our family was playing a role. We either helped her move toward recovery or stood in her way. Until we all became aware of the roles we were playing—enabler, persecutor, rescuer, or victim—we would interact in the same old ways, and nothing would change.

With this new understanding of the addict's personality and disease, I no longer allow myself to be manipulated or dragged down by the turmoil of her life.

TODAY I WILL look carefully at the role I've been playing, and then I will take the lead in my own life.

Enabling

We talk a lot in Families Anonymous about "enabling." What do we mean? We mean continuing to do those things that allow another person to remain "stuck" in the disease of addiction. Enabling means relieving someone of life's normal consequences, thereby short-circuiting the process of growth.

Enabling is my toughest character defect to give up. It is so easy for me to step in and "help," when I know I should step back and allow that other person room to grow by suffering the consequences of his own mistakes. At times when it would be convenient for me to offer help, I find it extremely painful to see my addict struggle alone, although he may be making progress in his own way.

I find it hard to allow him to suffer pain when I could ease that pain by my enabling. I sometimes think of him as a slow learner, yet when I realize how guilty I am of enabling, I think, "Who am I to judge another person?"

TODAY I WILL remember that when I relieve the pain, I only prolong the illness.

April 17

Helping or Controlling?

How easy it was for me to take over and direct someone I regarded as sick and unable to function! Even after my daughter was in recovery, I continued trying to engineer her life—under the guise of keeping her on the right track. I thought it was not only my right but my duty. Otherwise, what kind of parent would I be?

The key words are *helping* and *controlling*. Through participation in Families Anonymous, I've found there is a great difference between help and control. The notion of keeping someone on track denotes control. But I know now that I have no control over any other person.

I took a long, hard look at myself and realized I needed to change my attitudes and actions. To help my daughter, I had to let her go, with love.

My daughter does not need my lectures, threats, promises of rewards, or protection. She does need my encouragement, my faith that she can succeed, and my acceptance of her right to manage her own life.

TODAY I WILL let FA help me distinguish between help and control.

Helping

For me, one of the most difficult obstacles to full participation in the Families Anonymous program arose at the very onset of my involvement. I wanted desperately to help my child! How could I, a loving parent, not do things for her, especially since her use of drugs and alcohol seemed to make her so vulnerable and even more in need of help?

When I asked this question at FA meetings, the replies never satisfied me until finally I began to understand what my FA friends were trying to tell me. It gradually dawned on me that by doing things for my daughter, I was depriving her of the opportunity to experience the consequences of her behavior. So long as I kept it up, she would never have any reason to want to change her way of living.

Gradually I stopped doing and learned simply to be. I could be loving and caring without interfering in my child's decisions. I could be understanding, knowing that she suffers from a disease called alcoholism, and recognizing that only painful experience can motivate her to choose help to get well.

TODAY I WILL help by not interfering.

April 19

A Better Life

My husband and I are changed people since we joined the Families Anonymous program. Our new attitudes and behaviors have helped in all our relationships–with our son, extended family, friends, and even business acquaintances. We have also seen changes in our drug-dependent son, many of them for the better.

What are these changes? No longer do we blame ourselves for our son's problem or overreact to incidents in his life, even if we disapprove. We do not comment unless we are directly asked for our opinions. We no longer overprotect or criticize his lifestyle.

If he makes errors in judgment, he suffers the consequences. By the same token, when he makes the right decisions, he experiences pride and heightened self-esteem. We now realize that all of us have a right to choose how we want to live.

We have not abandoned our son. On the contrary, we are in constant communication. We give him our love, our encouragement, and our respect as a human being. Our relationship has improved a great deal.

TODAY I WILL enjoy the freedom that goes with a better way of life.

Guilt of a Single Parent

Before coming to Families Anonymous, I suffered from the "if only" disease. I constantly blamed myself: If only my children had a father in the house! If only I weren't a working mother! If only we had more money or lived in a different neighborhood! Many single parents suffer an inordinate amount of guilt about "short-changing" their children.

FA has taught me that I am not to blame when my child seems unable to cope with life on its own terms. Letting go of these guilt feelings helps me to live positively today and to maintain a more objective attitude as I deal with any crises that arise.

I have finally recovered from the "if only" disease. I have reprogrammed my mental "computer," eliminating guilt. But I may hang on to one "if only": If only everyone who needs Families Anonymous could discover its worth!

TODAY I WILL replace guilt with gratitude.

April 21

Expectations

Before I became familiar with the principles of Families Anonymous, my expectations often led to frustration and anger. When I placed all my expectations on others, they resented my attempts at manipulation. And my unreasonable expectations discouraged them from making improvements on their own. When my words and actions did not produce the desired results, I expressed my disappointment through alienation and anger.

What I've learned through FA has changed my attitude about *expectations*. Nothing is wrong with high hopes, but today I do not allow anything or anyone falling short of the mark to throw me into anger or despair. Instead, I allow others to work on their own shortcomings, while I devote myself to working on mine.

Today I know that change comes slowly. By keeping my expectations realistic, I minimize my disappointment in myself or others.

TODAY I WILL set aside expectations and leave the future to my Higher Power.

Spiritual Awakening

The Twelfth Step begins, *Having had a spiritual awakening as a result of these Steps....* These words really puzzled me when I first came to Families Anonymous. I wondered if I could expect a great enlightenment, complete with thunder or ringing bells.

For me, the awakening came about in small happenings. It was an awakening when, for the first time, I quietly said, "I love you but I can't help you. All you have to do is pick up the phone and call Alcoholics Anonymous or Narcotics Anonymous." I had a spiritual awakening on the first morning I looked out the window and thought, "What a beautiful day! I feel wonderful."

I knew further awakening when, during a meeting, I helped a newcomer toward peace of mind by sharing my growing experiences. When the Serenity Prayer pulled me through a difficult time, I could count that as yet another spiritual awakening.

TODAY I WILL be grateful for the miracle of small awakenings.

April 23

Step Twelve

Sometimes I feel reluctant to take Step Twelve. Am I afraid to encounter someone else's pain, lest I find that mine isn't as far behind me as I imagine? Have I really looked for someone who needs Families Anonymous? Do I really listen? Do I really see? Is my moment of sunlight too bright to include that person who is in the shadows and still hurting?

FA teaches me that my spiritual awakening overcomes despair and cynicism. It creates a need to share FA with others, instills a desire to help, frees me to feel compassion and understanding without judging. This awakening enables me to love, to forgive, to live and let live.

With courage, I can share my experience with those who still stumble in the dark. I can tell of my own awakening, then leave the results of my efforts to a Higher Power.

TODAY I WILL carry the message to others who seem to want it, granting them the dignity to receive it or leave it, as they decide.

Step Five

Admitted to God, to ourselves, and to another human being the exact nature of our wrongs.

When I admit my faults to God, to myself, and to another human being, it becomes clear that my shortcomings do not make me less worthy, only human.

Accepting my own frailties and imperfections allows me to accept, without judgment or condemnation, the faults and poor choices of others. Eventually, I am even able to share my human failings in Families Anonymous meetings, helping others to see that we've all made similar mistakes.

TODAY I WILL remember that making a mistake is being human. Trying to be perfect is "playing God."

April 25

Mistakes

After many years of living with an alcoholic husband, I had become about as passive as anyone could be. Without being conscious of it, I avoided taking any kind of action, for fear of *making a mistake*. My craving for perfection was keeping me from having any life of my own.

When my son went through treatment for chemical dependency, I was encouraged to attend Families Anonymous. Sharing in meetings, working the Steps, reading the literature—all these activities are helping me learn that it's all right for me to act, and even to *make mistakes!*

Human beings all make mistakes at times, and no one expects me to be superhuman. This new understanding has helped me a great deal in all my day-to-day relationships. How good it feels to grow!

TODAY I WILL live as fully as I can and count my mistakes as progress.

On Saying *No*

Through practice, I am learning to say *no*, undaunted by the anger of the addict in my household when he doesn't get his way. I work hard to overcome my anger at him and the lingering guilt I feel even when I know I've done the right thing.

When I look at his behavior rationally, I see that it comes from immaturity, heightened by misuse of drugs and a long history of getting what he wants.

Today I have an opportunity to change my responses to his behavior. I can stand up for myself and my values, say *no* when it's appropriate, and give him a chance to adjust to a recovering new me.

Having been a "doormat" for so long, I know it will take time, patience, and consistency for me to be able to say *no* and feel good about it.

TODAY I WILL congratulate myself when I am strong enough to say *no*.

April 27

Sarcasm

Before I came to this program, I used sarcasm to hurt, to get my point across, to get rid of my anger. I was hurting, and I wanted to hurt back.

After some time in the Families Anonymous program, however, I became aware of just how biting and hurtful sarcasm really is. It attacks self-esteem and destroys initiative. I decided there were better ways of dealing with those around me.

In learning to accept people as they are, I can catch myself now when I'm tempted to fall back on my old sarcastic ways. As I continue to work on my own inventory, a new awareness of my defects helps me to think before I speak.

When I say the Serenity Prayer, I ask for courage to *change the things I can*, and one of those things I *can* change is myself.

TODAY I WILL abandon sarcasm in favor of kindness.

Inventory

Before I came to Families Anonymous, I had lost all faith in myself as a parent and even as a worthy person. Overcome with guilt, remorse, and self-pity, I had gradually lost the respect of my children, my peers, and even myself.

Through the Fourth Step, FA has helped me see my faults, real and imagined. But beyond those faults, I have also discovered my assets. I have found much that needs to be changed. I've also found a lot in me that is good.

Focusing on new objectives has enhanced my self-esteem. Working on changing my attitudes has restored my initiative and respect for myself.

Grateful for these changes, I'm now able to reach out to others, both in and out of my group, with confidence that I can be of help in some small way.

TODAY I WILL identify one defect and work to change it; then I will look for an asset of which I can be proud.

April 29

Anger

In my opinion, the purpose of going to Families Anonymous is to gain peace and serenity.

One of the ways I do this is by backing away any time my "problem person" is angry. I've observed that regardless of what he's angry about, he usually vents his hostility on those who care about him most. He knows we will always forgive and love him, whereas strangers or mere acquaintances won't tolerate his attacks.

Today I choose never to accept verbal abuse or temper tantrums from the addict. After several years in FA, I am able to ask him serenely to leave my house if he starts to act out. When he becomes antagonistic toward me for any reason, I can tell him calmly that I choose to not speak any further.

At times I ask him to consider me a stranger when he speaks to me, because he would not be disrespectful toward a stranger. I try to let him know I will communicate with him at any time, so long as we can do so civilly and without anger toward each other. And I emphasize that I love him, even though I reject his angry attacks.

TODAY I WILL assert my right to serenity and respect.

Open Letter to a Child

Before Families Anonymous, I made it my responsibility to…
- be sure you associated with the "right" people
- see that you were in at a decent hour
- keep you from using drugs
- protect you from a cruel world
- dictate your behavior
- protect you from yourself and others
- endure your abuse

I did these things out of a misguided understanding of love, arrogantly believing I knew best, blaming myself for your unreadiness to face the world.

Through my Higher Power and FA, I learned that my responsibility actually is to…
- show you the map but let you plan your own life journey
- share my values but respect your right to yours
- let you fall so you can learn to stand up again
- set reasonable conditions for sharing my home with you
- communicate those conditions and see that they are met
- base my serenity on my own response to life, not on yours
- love you and myself unconditionally

TODAY I WILL keep my responsibilities clear, letting you take care of your own.

May 1

How Does Your Garden Grow?

We have been taught in Families Anonymous that the seeds planted by the program can be nourished only by us. So if you want to "bloom where you are planted," it's time to…
- encourage instead of discourage
- forgive instead of resent
- act instead of react
- pray instead of worry

These are the fertilizing agents for our newly planted "garden" where the fruits of hope, strength, and peace will grow.

TODAY I WILL cultivate my own growth instead of digging up old, useless pain.

Sobriety

Sometimes we wait anxiously for the "golden gate" of sobriety to open, not only for the sake of our loved ones but also for our own suppressed needs. And when that miraculous portal does open fully, we rush through it, energetic with responsibility. We may shower our recovering loved ones with gifts and rewards, basking in our own grateful relief. We assume we've reached our destination.

But isn't our system of rewards another form of control? Aren't we setting ourselves up as judges who determine when a person is worthy of privileges—or when he or she deserves to lose them?

These are dangerous waters for us *and* for those recovering from addiction. It's a sign that we are once again trying to become chief helmsmen of *their* vessels. Once again we are attempting to deny them the dignity of achievement and the growth of character that are the fruits of their own trials and errors.

In recovery, as well as in the days that precede it, our loved ones need to face life squarely. They must meet and deal with highs and lows, tests and woes, without our interference.

TODAY I WILL allow others to meet their own responsibilities, giving them credit as they learn to "paddle their own canoes."

May 3

Step One

My recovery starts with Step One of the Families Anonymous program. *I am powerless over drugs and other people's lives.*

But how daunting this seems! My child's behavior has dominated my life for so long that letting go is difficult to understand and even more difficult to do. In the name of love, I've tried to control this person for years.

Why do I persist in this fruitless effort? Am I afraid of being abandoned and alone? But am I not abandoned and alone anyway? Do I fear some tragedy if I'm not there to watch over my loved one, even though he does as he pleases anyway?

The Twelve Steps are clear: My own recovery starts when I accept the reality that I cannot control what happens to another person. My child's life belongs to him and no one else; my life belongs to me.

From the moment I accept these facts, I will begin to regain the essentials of life: honesty; right values; openness; friendship; time for me; faith; and, eventually, serenity and happiness.

TODAY I WILL acknowledge the reality of my powerlessness over others and work to change myself.

Let Go and Let God

It was wintertime in Chicago. My husband was recovering in Kentucky. I had three small children and no job. My heat had just been turned off.

I spent the morning at my neighbor's home, calling community agencies and hot lines. I got no help, no answers or referrals. I did get some wrong numbers. I tried relatives and friends. No one was home. I couldn't even get through to friends in Families Anonymous just to talk.

In desperation, I told God it was up to Him. I had tried everyone else and had gotten nowhere. To my surprise, a calm descended upon me. I had a fireplace and some wood; I lit a fire. God would help me. Fifteen minutes later, my neighbor came to tell me that I had a phone call. I heard welcome words: a long-overdue profit-sharing check had finally come in and would be delivered to me that evening.

Coincidence? To me, coincidence is God incognito.

TODAY I WILL turn my life over to my Higher Power and trust in His infinite wisdom.

May 5

Guilt

My mother and sister tell me I'm a brute because I don't rescue my chemically dependent, adult daughter from her own consequences. They think I should give her money for food or allow her to stay at my house when she has no place else to go. At times it seems that the whole world wants to lay a burden of guilt on my shoulders.

Families Anonymous has helped me realize that parenthood is not a popularity contest. I cannot win my daughter's love by supporting dependency. Nor can I win other people's approval of my parenting style. When guilt fostered by others makes me uncomfortable, I find it helps to call an FA friend. I know this friend will listen, share experiences, and possibly remind me of some Step or slogan to get me over rough times.

So long as I am working the Twelve Steps, following the program of FA, and seeking the direction of a Higher Power, I am doing the very best I can.

TODAY I WILL do for myself and others the things that lead to recovery rather than to others' approval.

Faith

Throughout my life, my faith in my Higher Power has always been strong. When my family difficulties reached such a point that I was utterly overcome by grief and confusion, I tried desperately to turn my family crisis over to my Higher Power. That's when my Higher Power led me to Families Anonymous.

Discovery of the program was an enlightenment. I learned that turning over my painful situation was much easier when I also *let go* of the problem. This was more difficult. But with my faith and some patience, I was able to focus my attention away from the pain and the situation and toward myself.

Gradually I learned to let go. Practicing the program has brought a daily growth in my own maturity and a new depth to my faith in my Higher Power.

TODAY I WILL rely even more fully on faith in my Higher Power, turning over to God the job I've tried unsuccessfully to do by myself.

May 7

Little Prayers

"God be with me (her, him). Thy will be done." This is one of my little prayers for desperate moments.

When faced with confusion, my little prayer is, "I'm listening, God. Please say something." If I get quiet and really listen, I usually discover a helpful idea to carry me through.

If caught up in anger and resentment, I sometimes say, "Thank you for this person I resent. No doubt he (or she) carries a message I need to hear."

There are other short prayers I rely upon:

"God, I'm caught in a 'traffic jam.' Please help me shift into normal."

"I'm on your side, God. Please help me remember you're on mine."

"God, help me get past the thorns to the rose."

"God, help me stand this pain a little longer, because I know you're trying to help me grow."

"God, please help me to listen to my inner voice."

"God, please give me what you think I need."

TODAY I WILL strive for conscious contact with my Higher Power through even a little prayer.

Silence

"I just kept my mouth shut." I hear this often at Families Anonymous meetings. Sometimes it's good to keep quiet. We're all learning how futile it is to plead, scold, and lecture.

However, I've noticed that just "keeping my mouth shut" often causes *me* to grind my teeth and act very hostile.

To avoid the pitfalls of pouting or giving someone "the silent treatment," I find it more constructive to detach myself from the one whose behavior disturbs me and to use my times of silence to ponder the program. I ask myself, "What Step applies to this situation?" or "What lesson does my Higher Power want me to learn from this?" Then I feel less tense, and perhaps others do too.

TODAY I WILL use silence as an opportunity to consider carefully the things I do and say.

May 9

Hate

I was shocked one day when I heard myself say of my own daughter, "I hate her." How could I—a mother who has always loved her child very deeply—say that? Was I speaking out of hatred, or was I speaking out of hurt in reaction to her destructive ways?

A call to my Families Anonymous sponsor helped me realize that it's really my daughter's actions and the disease of addiction that I hate. If I didn't love her, I would not feel this intense hatred for the disease that can destroy both her and our relationship.

The opposite of love is not hate. It's indifference. If we didn't care about the people we're concerned with in this program, we would not feel those extreme emotions toward our loved ones: love for them as persons, hatred for their destructive symptoms.

TODAY I WILL keep my hatred for addictive behavior grounded in compassion for the addict.

Step Two

Came to believe that a power greater than ourselves could restore us to sanity.

Sanity? What is sanity? Most of us couldn't recognize it, much less describe it. Little by little, day by day, our lives had become so twisted that sanity became a remote idea, certainly not within our grasp.

How sane were we when we took nightly inventory of our silverware or slept with our wallets under our pillows? How sane were we when we eagerly believed our children were holding pot for someone else? How sane were we when we threatened and yelled and used physical force to keep our children from drugs? How sane were we when we ourselves were frantic and out of control?

Once we can admit our lack of power, we are ready to accept a Higher Power, one we can turn to for restoration of our sanity. We hear others in our group who have come to depend on a greater power. We can see and admire their serenity and faith. Perhaps sanity is within our grasp after all!

TODAY I WILL take the brave step of trusting my Higher Power to help me detach from the insanity all around me.

May 11

Attitudes

At every Families Anonymous meeting I hear those wonderful words in the reading of HELPING, about changing *contempt for what he does to respect for the potential within him.*

It took a while in the program before I applied this concept to my own life and my own family. Once I was able to start looking for the potential within my daughter, I could give up trying to have power over her. I learned to check my contempt and say, "She may be doing things I don't like, but she's really a good person. She loves people. She's sensitive to the feelings of others."

When I became more tolerant of her mistakes and gave up trying to control her, she stopped being so defensive and gave up doing things to upset me. Both of us slip now and then, but I always remember to look for her potential—and my own. In so doing, I've gained much serenity.

TODAY I WILL increase my joy of living by looking for something to respect in everyone.

Expectations

We had expectations for our children as they were growing up. They had expectations for themselves as well. Some of those expectations were achieved, but then drugs, alcohol, and destructive behavior took over. Naturally we felt great disappointment in a son and a daughter who, it seemed to us, had let us down.

Through our son's recovery, we learned about Families Anonymous, a program for us. At our first meeting, I heard the words, *We admitted we were powerless over drugs and other people's lives, that our lives had become unmanageable.*

Powerless—that was a strong word! It was all I needed to hear. My children had to decide for themselves if and how they would meet any expectations. I had no power to change anything or anyone except myself; I had to work on me.

By attending two meetings a week and founding a new group in our town, I found the serenity necessary to carry on with my own life and make the changes I needed for myself, not for anyone else. Today I have expectations for myself alone.

TODAY I WILL encourage others to make their own progress in their own time, as I do the same for myself.

May 13
Wisdom

God, grant me the serenity to accept the things I cannot change, courage to change the things I can, and wisdom to know the difference.

How often we say this prayer at Families Anonymous meetings, but do we really hear the words and act upon the message? I know that all too often I forget to ask my Higher Power for the *serenity, courage,* and *wisdom* I need to deal with my day-to-day situations.

Before I joined FA, I led a highly disorganized life focused on my chemically dependent family member. Now it is time to focus on myself and my own choices.

Through repetition of and careful listening to this prayer, I am learning to put its words into action. And the added support of my FA group helps me develop a measure of serenity, courage, and wisdom, regardless of the actions of others.

TODAY I WILL say the Serenity Prayer and carry its words with me throughout the day.

Meetings

When things are going well, I'm tempted to skip my Families Anonymous meeting. It is so easy to begin thinking I can take care of my problems alone. I forget about the First Step and my powerlessness and slip back into my old ways of dealing with life. When I think I don't need a meeting, or when I feel too tired to go, that's probably when I need a meeting the most.

Going with a positive attitude, I can always gain something from a meeting. As I recover, I need always remember the Twelfth Step and how essential it is to share with others what I have been given.

When I first came into the program, I saw other members in various stages of recovery. Now, new people need to see me as I progress in my own recovery. Listening to newcomers reminds me that I've grown in the life of the program. The old-timers give me hope. When someone whom I thought had "made it" slips, I can forgive myself for my own slips.

TODAY I WILL keep my recovery alive and support the recovery of others by attending FA meetings.

May 15

Self-Pity

As soon as I realize I've relapsed into self-pity, I try to think of others who are worse off than I am. I can always find others in or out of the program who have it worse than I do. This makes me grateful for what I do have. Gratitude replaces self-pity and gets me back into recovery.

I have come to realize that I used to get a lot of secondary gain out of self-pity. My dramatic, poor-me monologues garnered attention and made others want to help. Another one of my subtle manipulations was to set up an image of myself as a rather superior person capable of shouldering great burdens, leading, I thought, to admiration on the part of those around me.

But members of my Families Anonymous group and study of the Twelve Steps helped me recognize these delusions. I was made aware of all these ploys, and I gradually gave them up, along with some of my other defects.

TODAY I WILL exchange self-pity for an attitude of gratitude.

Feelings

It's been said that resentments are just flattened-out anger, and that depression is anger gone underground. The family illness of addiction can certainly create all of these emotions.

Occasionally, a chemically dependent person's behavior may be worse after treatment. Family members are naturally frustrated, seeing the one they care about failing to use the tools he or she has been given.

When I allow my focus to stray back to the sick one in our midst, I make mountains out of molehills. I react, then feel guilty because I failed to follow my *own* program. Or I may do the opposite: I *don't* react. I "stuff" my feelings down inside, where they turn into resentment and self-pity.

In Families Anonymous, I've learned to deal with my feelings in a more positive way. I can decide how important an issue is. I don't have to accept intolerable behavior. I can choose to be angry and channel my anger in a way that doesn't tear someone else apart. I can defuse my emotions by calling a fellow member and talking out my feelings. Thus I avoid self-pity, resentment, and depression.

TODAY I WILL work with my feelings as I progress along the recovery road.

May 17

Reading Our Way to Recovery

Newcomers often ask why we have to hear the same readings at every Families Anonymous meeting. I wondered the same thing until, with continued attendance, the wisdom of the readings began to sink in.

In the beginning, unhappy and confused, I didn't really hear what they were telling me. Then I began to listen. With each repetition, I found some new phrase I hadn't heard before.

"Humbly asked Him…." Not until my second year in the program did I hear that I needed humility!

Often something has an entirely different meaning when I hear it for the fifteenth—or fiftieth—time. Perhaps it's timing; perhaps I listen better at a later meeting because my need for what I'm hearing is greater than it was at earlier meetings.

Now the readings have become deeply rooted in my consciousness. At times, when things aren't going well, a word or phrase from the now-familiar readings comes to mind and helps restore my serenity.

TODAY I WILL use one of the FA readings as a resource for recovery.

Anger

After the addict in my household came home from treatment, I went back to "walking on eggs," even though I knew better. Once again I tolerated behavior that was intolerable. I knew I shouldn't react. "Don't let it bother you," I kept telling myself. "She's sick."

But I continued to hold in my feelings of anger and hurt, until someone at a Families Anonymous meeting reminded me that accepting the unacceptable is sick too. This truth helped me get my priorities straight.

I was ready the next time my family member behaved in an unacceptable way. I said, "I don't like your behavior, and I'm not going to tolerate it." I felt much better because I'd spoken my true feelings instead of letting them fester inside of me.

Through FA, I have learned to be more tolerant and to not make mountains out of molehills, but I also have learned a better way to deal with my anger when something is a real "mountain."

TODAY I WILL find a useful way to confess and express my true feelings.

May 19

Taking Inventory

Blaming my situation on outside influences no longer makes sense, because Families Anonymous has shown me that I am powerless over other people, places, and things. I cannot change school systems, law enforcement agencies, or mind-altering substances. The only thing I can change is *myself.*

If I am to make that change for the better, I need to know which of my attitudes and reactions are making my life such a muddle of calamity and woe. I also need to know my strengths so that I can use them to make my life better. In the light of this understanding, I can see the importance of making a thorough inventory of myself in the Fourth Step and why I must continue the process as I follow the principle in Step Ten.

I'm not perfect, so I make plenty of mistakes. When I'm wrong, I aim to admit it promptly and take steps to correct my mistakes. When I learn from my mistakes, I grow in this program. I'm grateful for Steps Four and Ten and how they have changed my life.

TODAY I WILL use my inventory to help me find a better way to live.

Spirituality

In times gone by, I was often sad, even when I had no apparent reason to feel that way. Fortunately, my problems brought me into the Twelve Step way of living. After a year in the program, I realized my sadness arose from a need for deeper spirituality in my daily life. I had faith in a Higher Power, but it was an impersonal relationship.

Through this program, my faith has grown. I make conscious contact with my Higher Power every day, and all day, as I go about this business of living. My awareness and gratitude have multiplied tenfold. Few wonders, small or large, escape my attention and my praise or thanks. I can even find ways to love the seemingly unlovable people who cross my path.

I've learned to take criticism or negativity directed at me and make good use of them. I may be briefly uncomfortable with such occurrences, but then I remind myself, "There's something here my Higher Power wants me to hear." My "antenna" goes up, the "receiver" goes on, and I tune into some new truth about myself.

I am grateful that the troubles in my life brought me to Families Anonymous. I now have more joy than sadness because I am no longer spiritually starved.

TODAY I WILL keep constant contact with my Higher Power.

May 21

Obsession With People

Some of the people I love have a compulsive disease known as addiction. I have a similar compulsion: telling other people how to run their lives. I seem to be drawn to dysfunctional persons. Someone who has "no problems" is almost a bit boring to me.

However, I don't like my own compulsion, so the Families Anonymous program is just the thing to help me recover. Through studying the FA literature and reading other books about the need to control, I've devised a formula—CCHB—to help me realize when I'm "practicing my disease." Those letters tell me that trying to Control, Change, Help, or Blame another person is not a constructive way to behave.

Sometimes people are aghast when they hear me say that I must not help. But I define *help* as the *wrong* kind of help: paying other people's traffic tickets, doing things for them that they need to do for themselves, picking up after them, taking over their responsibilities. I need to know the difference between *serving* and being a *servant.*

TODAY I WILL give up my obsession for controlling other people and their lives.

Enabling Family Members

After I found the strength to let my drug-using daughter suffer the consequences of her behavior, some friends and relatives still tried to make me feel guilty.

Her grandmother and a favorite uncle were very hard on me when I refused to bail her out of jail. Grandma insisted on underwriting the legal costs of getting her grandchild out of difficulty, then allowed her to live in her home without contributing anything to the household.

My friends in Families Anonymous helped me to let go of this enabling family member. "She'll learn soon enough and probably end up asking your daughter to leave." The inevitable happened. Grandma gave up, but then Uncle took on the role of enabler. By then I'd learned to release everyone who chose to fall under my daughter's spell and help her remain sick.

Because of FA, I know that all the enablers will eventually fall away. Then my daughter will be forced to face herself and may or may not seek recovery. Meanwhile, I can only love her.

TODAY I WILL use my courage to resist enabling and let others find out for themselves how useless it is.

May 23

Minding My Own Business

At my first Families Anonymous meeting, I heard a member say, "I was feeling lousy this week. Then I realized it was because I really wasn't minding my own business."

His remark stuck in my mind, and I went through the following week questioning myself whenever I started to manage what other people were doing: "Is this any of my business?" Usually, the answer was, "No." I happily discovered that I had a lot more time and energy for my own concerns.

After that, I made a list of all the things that are my business: attending my FA meeting regularly; reading my FA literature; taking care of myself; being good to myself; taking time to make conscious contact with my Higher Power on a daily basis; keeping myself physically fit; looking as attractive as I can with what I have.

Perhaps my biggest job is *to love those around me enough to allow them to be whatever they choose to be.* It's simple but not always easy. With FA's help, it gets easier every day.

TODAY I WILL mind my own business. Doing so will keep me so busy that I'll have no time to tell others what to do.

Higher Power

Faith in a Higher Power has different meanings for different people. For some, it's trust in a particular divinity or religious teaching. Others come to accept the Families Anonymous meetings and members as their Higher Power. Some rely on the Twelve Steps. The Higher Power of my own understanding, I choose to call God.

When I first joined FA, I expected to learn from people who had been in the program for a while how to cure my addicted child. I prayed daily to God to grant me the strength and power to solve my drug-using child's problems. When no improvement took place, I felt God had let me down.

Then it occurred to me that I might be asking for help for someone who needed to ask for help for himself. Was this not an answer to my prayer? So then I asked God to help me understand and cope with my son's situation, and things were soon much better between us. I continued to offer encouragement but allowed him to seek his own solutions.

I continue to attend FA meetings, both for self-help and in the hope that in some small way I can help my fellow members or a newcomer in dire need.

TODAY I WILL pray *for knowledge of God's will for me and the power to carry that out.*

May 25

No Big Deal

After miserable years of struggling in the dark, I was finally told by a dear friend what was really wrong with my "problem" child. She told me my daughter very likely had a disease called chemical dependency and that it was fatal if not checked. I needed to do everything in my power to move her toward the specific help that she needed to get well. My friend also told me about Families Anonymous, where I could find recovery.

My gratitude to my friend is boundless. When my husband and I offered our daughter an opportunity for treatment, she accepted without hesitation. Her life was a mess. She knew how badly she needed help.

My friend has since become my "lifeline to sanity." Between meetings, when I get a little crazy, I telephone her; she always has the words of wisdom that I need to hear. One particularly irrational day, I dialed my friend's number and told her about my problem. Sure enough, she gave me her words for the day: "Don't sweat the small stuff."

"But how do I decide what's big and what's small?"

Her laughter carried clearly over the line. "The small stuff is everything you can't control."

TODAY I WILL consider what is and what is not important, and I will act appropriately.

Step Three

Made a decision to turn our will and our lives over to the care of God, as we understood Him.

A lot of us prayed a great deal. We prayed for peace and quiet. We prayed for strength to go on. Some of us prayed that our loved ones would stop using drugs—or would just get home safely at night. We prayed out of a sense of fear. There were many things to be afraid of—accidents, pain, even suicide.

In the Third Step, we find the antidote for our worries and fears. Here we can make that commitment to turn our will and our lives—*and* the lives of others—over to the care of God as we understand God. What a sense of freedom that brings! For me, it means laying down a terrible burden and starting to live my life, one day at a time, with the sure knowledge of God's loving care. I can "breathe easier" knowing that there is One I can turn to who is always there.

When we finally *let go and let God,* we can see how unbearable our lives were before we found this program. Peace of mind becomes more attainable once we decide to trust in our Higher Power. Our powerlessness is really a gift of freedom: freedom to love without fear, freedom to let go, freedom to let ourselves be healed.

TODAY I WILL choose the freedom found in Step Three.

May 27

Making Amends

After years of stress and frustration centered on my son's problems, I had a lot of anger. When I was angry at him, I was also short-tempered and critical of my husband. He didn't know what I was upset about because I didn't tell him. Sometimes he took the blame for my anger. Such displaced anger was unfair and harmful to everyone.

In working on Step Nine, I had to ask for my husband's forgiveness. I did this first by telling him that I realized what I had done and was sorry for the hurt I had caused him. I had to be humble enough and willing to look at my mistakes and to ask forgiveness for what I had done.

Making amends includes facing the reality, admitting the error, and then *changing the behavior*. Instead of hiding my anxiety and anger from my son and taking it out on my husband, now I tell both of them how I feel. I also try to be tolerant, understanding, and loving as a way of amending—*a mending* of relationships.

TODAY I WILL amend and mend my ways.

Serenity

When I came to Families Anonymous, my behavior and thoughts were distorted by fear, anger, and despair. I was living under intolerable conditions and didn't know there were alternatives. I didn't know I could choose to live any other way. Trying desperately to help my son, I didn't see my own need for help. I was allowing my drug-using son to determine how I felt. If he had trouble, I was anxious and fearful.

I found great release in coming to FA and meeting others who had had similar experiences and understood how I felt. Members of the group helped me find a better way to live. I've learned to give up trying to control my son's life. I've turned my concern for him and my own life over to my Higher Power, and in so doing I have found serenity.

TODAY I WILL guard my precious gift of serenity, not allowing the problems of others to disturb me.

May 29

Honesty

Honesty is surely an important factor in anyone's recovery. We, the family members, need to practice it just as much as does the addicted person we're concerned about.

As I grow in my ability to express myself honestly at Families Anonymous meetings and with my FA friends, I learn that it's possible to be honest at home with my family as well. The first is easier, but the second is also possible and even essential.

When I come to meetings willing to share my experiences and my shortcomings in total honesty, I can be sure of feeling better. My honesty may help someone else to be more honest too. When I am less than completely honest, I am delaying the progress of my own recovery and, perhaps, someone else's recovery as well.

TODAY I WILL be a little more honest than I was the day before.

Detach With Love

I was devastated when my drug-using son told me, "It's me and my drugs—or nothing at all!" I wanted him as a part of my life, but I also knew I could no longer take the emotional and mental abuse caused by his using.

From somewhere inside, I found the strength to say, "All right. I'll help you pack, and you can leave."

He left, but my anger and resentments remained. My frustrations nearly tore me apart. I fell into a deep depression and could see no way out. I had lost all self-respect, and I was an emotional wreck. Then I found Families Anonymous.

Through the FA program, I am learning to let go and release with love. The program is showing me that I have no reason to feel guilty for my decision. I cannot control my son's behavior, but I can control my own. I'm learning to act based on *tough love* and understanding instead of hatred and anger. FA has helped me release my son from my hands, into the hands of God.

TODAY I WILL trust that detaching with love is the best thing for my son and, most importantly, for me.

May 31

Guilt and Shame

When a crisis occurs in our family, I tend to assume all the blame. "It was my fault." "I should have…." "I'm not a good parent."

In my need to understand why things happen, I persecute myself. Filled with guilt and shame, I punish myself with critical thoughts. In my sense of inadequacy, I isolate myself, or else I hide behind a mask.

"Shame, shame on you!" That childhood taunt is a subtle background noise that only I can hear. An invisible finger points at me, instantly canceling any sense of my own worthiness.

But these accusations do not come from my Higher Power. My Higher Power is there waiting with open arms, waiting for me to be silent and hear, "You *are* worthy. You *are* lovable. You *are* uniquely human, and I love you more than you can ever imagine."

With love and forgiveness, my Higher Power greets and sustains me. It is one of the wonders of recovery that I am invited every day to let go of useless guilt and shame and allow love and forgiveness into my heart.

TODAY I WILL be still and listen for my Higher Power's message of comfort.

Step Four

Made a searching and fearless moral inventory of ourselves.

When we've been in a Families Anonymous program for a while, we can easily see the faults of others. We know when this one isn't being honest or that one isn't letting go.

But it's not so easy to analyze our own behavior. Maybe we've been so busy taking others' inventories, we haven't had time to take a clear look in the mirror. A few sarcastic remarks might have slipped out, or maybe we've been trying to manipulate someone again. Examining our behavior, attitudes, and ideals can make a big difference in our recovery.

How hard it is to view ourselves honestly, to dig down past the levels of denial and scrape away the hypocrisy. It's painful to face our foolish actions and downright stupid reactions. But wait! There have been times when we did something right, when we tried to overcome some bad traits. There were times when we were kind, generous, and loving, times when we did the best we could. A thorough inventory of ourselves has to include our good points too.

TODAY I WILL be honest with myself and others about my strengths as well as my weaknesses.

June 2

Toward Self-Improvement

> Appreciation is a wonderful thing. It makes
> what is excellent in others belong to us as
> well.
>
> —Voltaire

Envy and resentment of someone else can warp and
retard my quest for personal growth, whereas the
appreciation of another person's talents can inspire me
to nurture my own potential.

When I first began to attend Families Anonymous
meetings, appreciation of others was not a part of my
life. Only after working and reworking Steps Four
and Ten did I begin to appreciate the good in others,
even in my chemically dependent children. I learned
that the resentment and blame I placed on everyone
in my life only held me back from becoming the truly
fulfilled person I *could* be.

As I work at replacing my negative traits of envy
and resentment with love and acceptance, I also learn
to forgive myself. With the help of the Twelve Steps, I
can strive to improve. FA literature on Step Ten says,
"…we continue to work on ourselves."

TODAY I WILL strive to improve myself, using the
accomplishments of others to inspire me.

Marriage Survival

When a family suffers from the disease of chemical dependency, heartbreak and tragedy are frequently the result. Often one of the greatest sorrows is a rift between parents.

If parents allow themselves to be pitted one against the other and lose sight of the fact that they are partners as well as *parents,* the marriage may suffer severely. Touching base and communicating with each other become so difficult that a couple can fall into a pattern of seeming not to need each other. As conflicts and suffering escalate because of the drug use within the family, marriages and homes become battlegrounds.

But at some point, the children will grow up and leave home, recovering or not, and then there will be only *the two of them.* This may be a moment of great opportunity. A troubled couple may choose to seek help in understanding and overcoming the negativity and addictive disease in the family.

TODAY I WILL do my part to make the rest of our family life as loving as I can.

June 4

Laying Down the Burden

When I came to my first Families Anonymous meeting, I carried a heavy burden, a tightly clutched bundle of anger, hurts, and fears. I was suspicious and very much alone.

I thought I wasn't ready to give up that burden. It was all I had! I clutched it tightly to my chest. The longer I stayed in FA, though, the more difficulty I had holding on to this terrible load. I shifted it from arm to arm as welcoming hands reached out to me. It got in the way of the warm hugs I was receiving. Soon I found I had to set it briefly aside so I could hug back. Eventually I had to share it, because my FA friends wouldn't let me carry it alone. When I finally opened my arms fully to others, the burden dropped away altogether.

TODAY I WILL watch for a newcomer burdened by an intolerable load and stretch out my arms to lighten it. Here's a hug! Pass it on!

Dealing With a Disease

Our primary purpose in Families Anonymous is to *help those concerned with someone who has a problem of drug abuse or dependence.* We are here to lend support as we try to survive in the backwash of addictive illness.

Chemical dependency—alcoholism or addiction—is an ugly disease. It can ruin the lives of fine young men and women who began with great expectations. It causes hurts, frustrations, disappointments, and anger. We family members are sad for our addicts and ourselves.

We can wallow in self-pity. We can angrily blame our children, the schools, drug pushers, the law, society, even the recording industry. *Or* we can begin to recognize and deal with our feelings, gain knowledge about the disease, and take positive action to get our lives in order. No one else will do this for us. We can become responsible for our own recoveries.

As we gain strength by taking positive action in our own lives, we become better able to help others struggling with the same disease. We accept our troubled loved ones and support their changing attitudes and actions. We grow to love them again, separating them from the disease and the actions it precipitates.

TODAY I WILL be grateful for the understanding I have gained in FA and share that understanding with someone else.

June 6

FA—A Lifetime Program

When I first came to a Families Anonymous meeting, it was to learn how to cope with my son's use of alcohol and drugs. Over time, working the FA program, I changed and he changed. Our home was no longer a battlefield.

The question for me then was, "Do I still need to attend FA?" The answer was a very clear YES—for several reasons.

First is the newcomer. If I stopped attending meetings, how could I share my experience, strength and, most of all, hope with a newcomer? I shudder to think how I would have fared if no one had been at *my* first meeting.

I also need meetings to help me follow the Twelve Steps as my way of life. I try to use the FA principles, the Steps, and the slogans in every relationship: with my husband, relatives, friends, co-workers, and neighbors. It's true the Twelve Steps work when we are hurting from a loved one's destructive behavior, but in fact they work *all the time.* The more meetings I attend and the more I use the program, the easier it becomes to practice these principles in all my affairs.

TODAY I WILL continue my lifetime program in Families Anonymous.

Laughter

"At Families Anonymous meetings, we learn to laugh together about the things we used to cry over alone."

When I first heard that said at an FA meeting, I thought, "These people are crazy! How can they laugh about all the scary, horrible things that are going on in their lives?" Such things were no laughing matter in my life at the time.

After a while, I found that I too could laugh. Laughter became part of the healing process. All my frustration, anger, and guilt slowly faded away as members shared their experiences, strength, and successes, large and small. Eventually I could even laugh at myself when I saw what I was doing to myself by being so serious all the time.

Yes, there are those scary moments, but as I apply the FA program in my life, they seem to lessen, and sometimes now I can even laugh about the problem that first brought me to FA.

TODAY I WILL keep my sense of humor alive and well.

June 8

Miracles

When I walked into my first Families Anonymous meeting, it was to find out how I could change my son and stop his destructive behavior. After I attended meetings for a while and put the FA program into action, my son did make changes in his life—not because I changed him, but perhaps because I changed myself.

A "miracle" happened when I got out of the way and let my son take responsibility for his own actions. I worked my program for myself, instead of concentrating all my time and energy on what someone else was doing or not doing. I realize that I had blocked the way for my son's Higher Power to reach him, because I had always been "on the job."

It doesn't happen overnight, but by attending FA meetings regularly, calling or e-mailing other members, and reading the FA literature, letting go does become easier, little by little, one day at a time.

TODAY I WILL let go and watch a "miracle" happen.

Step Three

In Steps One and Two of the Families Anonymous program, we are encouraged to admit that *our lives are unmanageable* and that *a power greater than ourselves can restore us to sanity.*

The first admission I made grudgingly. The second was even more difficult, since I often believed I was the only one in my chaotic household who was still sane.

Step Three invited me *to turn my will and my life over to the care of God, as I understood Him.* I had to turn it over to *God*—not Santa Claus. Until then, I'd been telling God to turn His will over to me: "Make him stop using drugs. Make him do right. Make him turn his life around." That was *my* will talking, not God's.

Instead of continuing to "write letters to Santa Claus," I finally learned to listen for what my Higher Power is directing me to do. Making such a decision is a life-changing action. The night after I finally began to let go, I slept peacefully for the first time in years.

TODAY I WILL give thanks for a helping Higher Power and entrust myself to that Power anew.

June 10

Responsibility

For a long time, my children and I struggled together in family therapy. Every week we agreed to try not to fight and argue, but we always failed.

Then I found Families Anonymous, where parents work to solve their own problems. I learned what *my* responsibilities are and what responsibilities belong to my children, and the fighting stopped.

I learned that it wasn't my responsibility to get my kids out of bed in the morning, so my yelling ceased. I found that their laundry is their responsibility, so I no longer complained about retrieving their dirty clothes from under their beds.

I had always been embarrassed if they didn't look well-groomed. What would people think of *me*? I wasn't concerned for the kids but for *myself*. Now I see that if they wear dirty clothes, it's not a reflection on me. Many things we fought about had to do with how I thought I would appear to the outside world.

Laundry soap, bicycles, and most gadgets come with instructions. Kids don't. I have to rely on on-the-job training for life and parenthood. My best "instruction manuals" are the other parents in FA and the FA literature.

TODAY I WILL establish healthy responsibilities by following the FA way.

Communication

How often have you asked someone to do something, only to discover they've done it wrong? Who or what was the problem?

All people don't hear or understand things the same way I do. When I talk to someone, my communication must be very clear and straightforward. I cannot assume that my conversation or writing will automatically be understood. Instead, I need to give others a chance to ask questions and to respond. Then I can be sure they understand how to do what's expected.

I know what I mean, but sometimes I need to listen to what or how I say things, then ask myself, "Did I say that in a way another person can understand?"

I must consider the person I'm talking to and make sure I communicate on his or her level, in his or her terms. Sometimes I need to ask, "Do you understand?"

TODAY I WILL be careful to say what I mean in a polite, clear, loving manner, with consideration for the understanding and feelings of others.

June 12

Daily Inventory

In order to see beyond the negatives in my life, I find that writing a list of the positives helps me appreciate how far I've come. It also gives me a point of reference as I do a daily Tenth Step. I think over what I've accomplished this day, both in practical terms and spiritual growth. Did I finish what I started? Was I kind to those around me? Was I good to myself? Did I take time to contact my Higher Power?

Listing my attributes as well as my defects of character gives me some balance and shows me how much I've grown. Daily inventory keeps me humble and grateful. This is much better than dwelling on angers, resentments, fears, and self-pity.

TODAY I WILL take stock of how far I have come, think positively, and let go of the past in order to live fully today.

From Mourning to Recovery

When I first learned my daughter was chemically dependent, I felt as though she had died. All the dreams I had for her were gone. I was truly in mourning.

I could not recover until I allowed myself to feel that grief and then work through it. Although I still fall back into mourning occasionally when I see that she is using, my dream now is for her recovery. When and if she becomes ready, her life will bloom again.

As for me, I've moved ahead with my own recovery. The Families Anonymous program tells me that I must make my own life bloom, regardless of whether or not another chooses to get well.

TODAY I WILL dry my tears and work for my own recovery.

June 14

Real Choices

My biggest character defect is wanting my own way, especially where my kids are concerned. There are times when I get home from work tired and don't want to cook. I tell the kids we'll eat out, and I ask where they want to go.

In the past, I might have given them a choice of two places, but if they picked the place that wasn't my first choice, a big argument followed, and we wound up going where I wanted to go.

Now that I live by the Families Anonymous program, I give them a choice that really is a choice; then I do my best to keep my big mouth shut. I can even let someone stay home and have a peanut-butter-and-jelly sandwich. Now when I ask someone to choose, I really allow that person the freedom to do so.

I also know I have a right to be the one to choose.

TODAY I WILL remember that I can make choices, but when I offer that privilege to another, I will abide by that person's wishes.

Opportunities

I recently heard a taped lecture for business people on cultivating positive attitudes. That's something I really need to do. The lecturer said that many people come to business meetings thinking in terms of problems, and that's depressing. I often come to Families Anonymous meetings focused on problems too; *that's* depressing.

A better way to approach any meeting is in search of an opportunity. Every problem presents an opportunity for growth and change.

What a good way to look at life! Life is full of opportunities to try new ideas, new solutions. Every crisis is an opportunity for me to do better. I must have had a long way to go because I've had so many opportunities to do better!

TODAY I WILL gratefully accept the opportunities life presents for me to grow.

June 16

Gratitude

It's difficult to forgive those who have hurt us, let us down, or left us feeling degraded. We cling to our bitterness against them. Such feelings fill up time that could be spent enjoying music, viewing a fine painting, or hiking in the woods. How good it would be if we could get rid of the bad memories and hurts!

What can we do about our hurts and disappointments? FA has given me the tools to help me rise above them. The program encourages me to let go of resentments by concentrating on gratitude. Sometimes I even make lists of my blessings.

I've also learned in the program and through my improved conscious contact with a Higher Power to place *everyone* in God's hands. I know that if I cannot forgive those who have hurt me, God can.

TODAY I WILL overcome my hurts by focusing on my blessings.

Expectations

Before we came into this program, many of us were confused, bewildered, and angry about the problems that plagued our lives with a drug-dependent person.

Through Families Anonymous we learned that…

• We did not cause the problem.
• Drug dependence is an illness, not a moral failure.
• We cannot cure or control our loved one's illness.

One of the major stumbling blocks to our personal recovery may be our own expectations. Whether our chemically dependent loved ones are recovering or still suffering, we can make sure that we don't try to control their behavior by our expectations. For if those expectations are not met, we will be setting ourselves up for anger, hurt, and resentment.

We cannot establish goals for others. We *can* turn the focus on ourselves. Through FA groups, the Twelve Steps, and our Higher Power, *we can change ourselves. Others we can only love.*

TODAY I WILL keep my expectations realistic and apply them only to myself.

June 18

Criticism

Sometimes I think I have a right to complain about family members and the way things went today. Don't I have a right to feel sorry for myself?

If I am serious about my recovery, the answer is no. Now that I am part of the Families Anonymous program, I am learning to give up being miserable.

Being a chronic complainer is a terrible, destructive way to live. If we are always critical instead of loving, we destroy each other. Rather than making a career of fretting, we can accept FA's invitation to nurture ourselves and our own improvement.

TODAY I WILL silence my critical thoughts and get on with living the recovery way.

Know-It-All?

No one is more impossible to deal with than a know-it-all, whether it's an alcoholic or drug abuser who won't admit the problem or a person who thinks everyone else is wrong. It's frustrating and exhausting to try to help someone who is self-righteous and believes he does not need to change his ways.

Yet we ourselves may not have all the answers either. We too need to grow and change certain patterns of behavior. Maybe we should listen carefully to criticisms and suggestions, whether said kindly or unkindly.

It's very possible that our Higher Power may be using our critics to call us to a change of heart.

TODAY I WILL humbly pray for guidance, humility, and the courage to change what needs to be changed in myself.

June 20

More Little Prayers

Long and short prayers written by others are often a comfort to me. I also like to make up my own little prayers because they feel more sincere and personal. Here are a few.

"Make me an instrument of your will and a channel of your love."

"Temper my words with your kindness, and soften my voice with your grace."

"Here I am with all my flaws. I give myself and those I would help into your loving care."

"Okay, God, if that's what you want for him/her/me, I can accept it."

"God, I think I'm doing the footwork. Can you give me a hand?"

"Whatever!"

"God, help me to love this person rather than to try controlling or changing him."

"Help me confess my resentment of another in a way that helps both of us."

"God, give me the knowledge, strength, and awareness to be what you would have me be."

"God, thank you for this day."

TODAY I WILL find a way to pray.

Manipulations

For some of us, being pushy comes far too easily. Almost instinctively, we find ourselves gloating over others, nagging, criticizing, and threatening them with exclusion or the silent treatment if they don't give us our way. We love to "play God"!

Families Anonymous helps us resist this impulse to dominate or control other people's lives in any way. Doing so is easier when we take an honest personal inventory of ourselves and discover the subtle ways in which we try to manipulate people. Knowing how unpleasant I find others' attempts to "con" and manipulate me, I've resolved to work especially hard at overcoming any tendency to behave in the same way. With humility I can ask God's forgiveness and then forgive myself for my self-deceiving ways.

TODAY I WILL ask my Higher Power's help in resisting the temptation to manipulate others.

June 22

The Frets

Once there was a family I'll call the Frets; that's all they ever did. Mr. and Mrs. Fret spent thousands of dollars on their chemically dependent son Tommy, and they spent all their energy trying to straighten him out. They could talk of nothing else.

Finally, a wise therapist said, "Your whole life is wrapped up in the sick kid. Families Anonymous might be just what you need."

The Frets grew stronger as they applied the FA program to their lives. They made a pact to not speak of Tommy for one whole day. Succeeding in that, they rewarded themselves with another day free of fretting. One day at a time, they refrained from worry.

Tommy continued to refuse their offers of help for his illness. When it became clear they could no longer tolerate his behavior in their home, they found the courage to ask 19-year-old Tommy to move out. After that, they began to rebuild a life together, based on the Twelve Steps.

Although Tommy went from bad to worse, the Frets only said, "We love you, but we cannot solve your problems." It wasn't easy to see their son wandering the streets under the influence of drugs. In the end, their strength and patience paid off. Today, young Tom still has problems, but he is clean and sober.

TODAY I WILL love and respect my addicted family member by letting him work out his own life.

Success in FA

Success in the Families Anonymous program is not measured by whether or not we "get them clean and sober." That's often a hard concept for newcomers to grasp—it was for me. But after some time of working this program, I learned that whether my dear one recovers from addiction or not, I have a life to live.

I also have choices to make that will lead to my own life being miserable or comfortable. I can choose to hang on to my obsessive concern for a person bent on apparent self-destruction. Or I can choose to look to my own growth, my work, my recreation, my joys, and my serenity. Those are the *true* measures of success.

TODAY I WILL work at building a successful life for *myself.*

June 24

You Can't Push the Stream

On a warm summer day, I sat beside a stream in the woods. Wistfully, I asked, "How long, oh God, how long?" Friends in Families Anonymous had said, "This too shall pass." But I was impatient.

I listened to the brook and watched as the water eddied and flowed. Surface reflections of sun and sky changed constantly, but the water flowed along at an unchanging rate.

Then I thought, "I can't push the stream. It flows by itself. I really am powerless."

I realized then that I could not push the flow of life around me either. I could only move along with it. It is reassuring to know I don't need to direct that flow. Even more reassuring is the fact that I have a "boat" and some "oars" to help me navigate the rest of my journey—my Twelve Step program.

TODAY I WILL keep both oars in the water: my program and a conscious contact with my Higher Power.

It Works If You Work It

At the end of most Families Anonymous meetings, you hear, "Keep coming back. It works." I always add, "…if you work it."

What does *working the program* mean? It means reading something every day about the Steps and other principles in our FA literature.

It means searching out the source of my uncomfortable feelings. Am I doing something that is counter to the program? Maybe I'm getting too involved in someone else's affairs. What Step do I need to study and think about?

Working the program means calling an FA friend to talk through a problem or express some anger. Or perhaps my friend is hurting, and I can be a good listener. Maybe I have some good news to report, a joy to share. It's not all trouble and woe, I know.

Working the program means attending and participating fully in meetings. Only by giving it away can I keep what the FA program has given to me.

Working the program means claiming whatever Higher Power I can and turning over my struggle to the help of that Power, through daily prayer and meditation.

TODAY I WILL work my program and share it with another.

June 26

Sponsorship

Early in my Families Anonymous program, there was a particular person who always told me what I needed to hear. This person often gave me a new way of seeing things. I spoke to him privately and asked him to be a sponsor for my wife and me. He agreed to sponsor me but suggested that my wife choose her own mentor.

Now I have had the honor of being asked to sponsor someone else. Am I really ready or capable of doing this important service? My sponsor says I am and urges me to take up the challenge. He assures me I will remember how his sponsorship worked—and the times when it didn't work, when he got too involved in my problems or tried to make things easier for me.

I believe my sponsorship will succeed if I *listen carefully, refrain from giving advice, and share what has worked for me* in my relationships with others.

TODAY I WILL humbly and gratefully accept the challenge of sponsoring or being sponsored by an FA friend.

Asking for Help

Children go through a stage that is all too familiar to a parent: "I can do it by myself!" We watch them struggle to climb the stairs, tie their shoes, button their buttons, and do all the other routine tasks of living.

When a parent takes over and does these tasks for the child, the jobs may get done in half the time, but the child's dignity suffers. Testing our knowledge and skills is the only way we grow in self-esteem, self-reliance, and self-discipline. A steadying hand can sometimes be very important, but most of the time, joy and self-confidence come only after a person has accomplished a task primarily through his or her own resources.

I need to allow my youngsters to do as much for themselves as they can, lest I rob them of opportunities for growth. A few failures along the way teach children more than does any amount of effort on a parent's part.

Doing it by myself is not a good idea, however, when I am struggling with the family disease of addiction. I am blinded by denial and my own defenses. Asking for help is all-important. When I found the courage to name my family's problem and ask for help, the situation began to turn around.

Doing it by oneself is essential for the child learning to live. Doing it by oneself is bad medicine for anyone who wants to learn the skills of recovery.

TODAY I WILL acknowledge that it's okay to ask for help.

June 28

FA Readings

When I was new to the Families Anonymous Twelve Step program, I wondered why we spent so much time reading the same materials at every meeting. I even came late to some of the meetings to avoid what seemed like a tedious ritual to me.

One night I was hurting so much that I went early to talk to someone on a one-to-one basis. That night I couldn't avoid the readings. I guess my Higher Power opened my ears, because the readings sounded completely new to me and full of meaning.

...we are powerless over drugs and other people's lives...

The compulsive use of drugs or alcohol does not indicate a lack of affection for the family.

I can change myself. Others I can only love.

Anonymity is the spiritual foundation of all our Traditions, ever reminding us to place principles above personalities.

These ideas no longer fall on deaf ears. Now I listen eagerly to all the readings, knowing that some of the hurt I'm harboring will begin to heal if I listen.

TODAY I WILL listen for the messages my Higher Power sends my way.

One Day at a Time

The greatest lesson I have learned in Families Anonymous is to take *one day at a time.* Along with the other slogans, the Steps, and the Traditions, *one day at a time* has given me back my emotional, physical, and spiritual life.

No longer am I consumed with the lives of those around me, with yesterday, with tomorrow. What personal freedom there is in no longer being obsessed! There would have been little recovery for me, had I not been helped by FA to reduce my chaotic life to *one day at a time.*

By allowing this and all the FA slogans to guide me, I have been led through the Twelve Steps, which, in turn, have led me to serenity, sharing, and caring.

TODAY I WILL remember to live just *one day at a time.* This day is precious to me.

June 30

No More!

I used to say, "Some days it just doesn't pay to get out of bed!" or, "I guess this is going to be one of those days."

Back then, I could while away the time with a catalog of my woes and a chronicle of how I had been mistreated. I could conjure up catastrophic expectations by the score.

But now that I've been in a Twelve Step program, I have better things to do with my day. If there are problems, I ask myself, "What can I do about them?" If there are constructive actions I can take, I move ahead to take them with as much courage as I can muster. Insoluble "nuts" are left to my Higher Power to "crack."

Having taken those constructive steps, I then go about my day, enjoying the special moments that come through living for NOW.

TODAY I WILL abandon self-pity and live for today.

Courage

Sometimes it takes more courage to be weak than to be strong.

In many a family living with impending crisis, there is the self-proclaimed Pollyanna who tries to keep a stiff upper lip, a calm head, and an optimistic smile in the face of growing chaos. There is usually someone else who evades reality, a Don Quixote, insisting there are only windmills to conquer by himself when it is increasingly obvious something far more serious and unmanageable threatens the family.

What seems like courage may really be a form of evasion or denial. If I am the Pollyanna or the Don Quixote, I know that behind my mask of denial, my illusion of self-sufficiency, there really cowers a frightened, helpless person. The first step to recovery is confronting the depths of those secret fears, for then I can join the rest of the human race and reach out for help for myself.

TODAY I WILL call upon my courage to admit how painful and overwhelming this family disease really is.

July 2

Responsibility

As newcomers to Families Anonymous, we find it difficult to accept the First Step—admitting we have no control over someone else, especially our own children. We find it difficult to believe we can do nothing to overcome the acts of our sons or daughters. "Why," we ask, "should we not be able to control our children's actions? Isn't that our responsibility as parents?"

Sometimes it takes Step Two to help us realize how much is beyond our control. We begin to understand how our own reactions may have actually made matters worse. Faith in *a Power greater than ourselves* helps us stop fretting. With few if any alternatives, we start to get ready for Step Three, in which we *let go and let God.*

In FA, we learn to recognize where our own responsibilities begin and end. We allow others to discover the same boundaries of responsibility for themselves.

TODAY I WILL accept my powerlessness over others and claim responsibility for myself.

Strength

On days when I feel that I have little strength, I pray for help. I want someone or something to assist me in dealing with my pain, fear, and emptiness.

As I pray, the strength does come. I don't know where it comes from. I only know that I sense a Higher Power, and whatever that power is, it gives me the courage to go on. I entrust myself to that power as I begin to take action or make decisions.

The person whose disease brought me to the Families Anonymous program will have to find strength on his own. Each of us finds this power alone, but finding it is truly a miracle.

The power is within me, outside me, and everywhere I look. The strength it brings is also within me, outside me, and all around.

TODAY I WILL face life with strength found through prayer.

July 4

Freedom

Our group pondered the meaning that each of us found in the word *freedom.* Here are the results:

Letting go of another's problems gave me a *freedom* I hadn't experienced before. I no longer had to waste time worrying about what might happen. I was free to work on my own recovery and happiness.

Freedom is looking in the mirror and smiling; it's liking who I am.

I find *freedom* when I turn my problems over to God.

Freedom comes through acceptance. When we learn to accept, we are relieved of despair and confusion.

Freedom is mine when I take Step One and accept my powerlessness.

Freedom is having faith in others.

Freedom is letting go of my own shortcomings.

Freedom is the opposite of the bondage I endured when I took on other people's problems.

I gain *freedom* when I draw up my own bill of rights and stand up for those rights.

Freedom is releasing others to suffer their own hurts, seek their own solutions, and live their own lives. By releasing them, I gain the *freedom* to live my life as my Higher Power directs.

TODAY I WILL become truly free by refusing to live through somebody else.

Hope and Encouragement

It's hard, at first, to come into the Families Anonymous program. We don't want to admit that our lives are in shambles and all our efforts have backfired. When I came to my first FA meeting, I thought no one in the world had ever been as miserable as I. At that meeting, I just cried aloud and voiced all the pain that had built up inside me.

But a seed was sown at that meeting too, and somewhere in the dim recesses of my awareness, I began to recognize the acceptance and understanding offered by the people in that FA group. New hope sprang up within me that just possibly I might someday be restored enough (as the others obviously were) to be able to risk loving again.

I had a new sense that I might once again know the joy of a relationship that had been lost with the seeming rejection of my children, whose problems had brought me to that meeting.

TODAY I WILL find hope, encouragement, and serenity in my FA group, rather than expecting family members to make me happy.

July 6

Step Five

Admitted to God, to ourselves, and to another human being the exact nature of our wrongs.

Taking a fearless look at myself wasn't as bad as I had anticipated. In doing Step Four, I found many good traits as well as some things I could change.

The next Step sounded a lot harder. As a former "perfect person," I found it hard to admit I had faults, much less admit them to anyone else.

I was always impressed by the honesty of the people in Families Anonymous. Many times I heard things I could really relate to and things I needed to hear. When certain character defects were shared, I could empathize and forgive. Yet I knew it would take a real act of faith for me to share *my* wrongs with someone else. I didn't like risking the loss of another person's respect.

But what a wonderful feeling it was finally to drop that mask of perfection. Soon my carefully built defenses broke down, and I could share reality with someone. My terrible wrongs weren't so bad after all!

Now I can share with my sponsor or my group how silly and mean and nasty I have been, knowing they will accept me just the same.

TODAY I WILL invite another person to help me heal.

Whose Way?

Prescribing what's best for another, no matter how comfortable and secure I may be in that knowledge, is not the Families Anonymous way. In fact, doing so under the guise of parental responsibility can be a cover-up for egotism and arrogance.

I may see myself as generally pleasant, friendly, sociable, hardworking, deeply caring—all traits and values that are highly regarded in general. Yet the son, daughter, or spouse who I hope will appreciate these qualities may turn away and say, "No, thanks. Your way is not my way; I'll pursue my own course."

This feels like rejection, and it is painful. It seems as though the guidelines and signposts that have directed my life are being thrown into question. My first response might be, "But look how well these guidelines have worked for me!" Often I cling desperately to this response; letting it go would mean admitting that my way is not the only way—and not necessarily the best way for another person.

In Families Anonymous I'm learning to work a program for myself, mapping a course into uncharted territory. My Higher Power has the ultimate direction for me. My job is to discern that way and follow it.

TODAY I WILL guide my steps along the path to serenity and encourage others to find their own way.

July 8

Isolation

I used to feel like a wounded dog, isolating myself, waiting to be healed. Since I've come to Families Anonymous, I feel like a human being again, in spite of unsolved problems. I've stopped trying to control or take responsibility for other people's choices. I love my daughter very much, but I can't live her life for her or know what motivates her actions.

I've put the spotlight back on my own life and come out of my isolation. I'm busy renewing old friendships and developing new ones. If I see someone who is suffering alone, I try to bring him or her the FA message of hope.

I've put the focus back on my whole family as well. By expressing our feelings of love for and acceptance of one another, we find our relationships beginning to heal, and we're enjoying each other's company again. I even feel more relaxed with my chemically dependent daughter. Although all our problems haven't disappeared, there are more peaceful times at home.

I am grateful to my Higher Power for leading me to FA and the Twelve Steps. My heart is healing at last.

TODAY I WILL thank my friends in FA for bringing me out of my small world of suffering and showing me a better way to live.

Service

I found the concept of service in Families Anonymous difficult to accept at first. It was all I could do just to get to a meeting! There were so many new ideas to absorb, so much to learn, and so much to *do.* There was little left of me for service.

Besides, there were all those "old-timers." Why didn't they volunteer? Gradually it dawned on me that these people had probably served a great deal already and were deliberately holding back to let the new ones get involved.

One of the earliest signs of my recovery was my growing willingness to give service to the group, even if it was just getting there early to make coffee. Taking on the responsibility of bringing doughnuts showed more improvement. When I finally realized that unless everyone helped, there would be no group, I was well on the way to healing. Using my energy to serve others was a great deal better than dwelling on my own self-pity and misery. Soon I was well enough to take on the job of passing out literature. Who knows where this will end?

Some day, I hope to be one of those "old-timers," who share encouragement and hope while giving newcomers an opportunity to serve the group and grow. For now my peace of mind depends upon giving whatever service I can to FA.

TODAY I WILL serve FA to the best of my ability.

July 10

Feelings

I used to be so busy trying to control and fix everybody else that I was hardly aware I had any feelings about anything. That was before I came to Families Anonymous.

The FA program has taught me I am responsible only for myself. Knowing this gives me time to do many things just for me. I can use some of the newfound time to recognize feelings as they arise.

I find it pleasant to acknowledge my new feelings of love, joy, and serenity. I also give myself permission to feel anger, for this can be a healthy feeling too if dealt with appropriately. No longer do I have to suppress my feelings. Even fear can be faced and worked through, with help from other members of FA.

Nowadays I even experience the luxury of having fun when I feel like it!

TODAY I WILL take the time to acknowledge my feelings and allow them to enrich my life.

The Serenity Prayer

What a great resource the Serenity Prayer is! It can help me cope with almost any situation.

When I first started attending Families Anonymous meetings, I just repeated the words because it was part of the program. Little by little, however, those words became *real* to me.

When I learned to accept the things I could not change, my mind became calm enough to reflect on the things that *could* be changed.

The Serenity Prayer's principles can be applied to any situation: financial burdens, fear of nuclear war, a cheating spouse, rebellious adult children, or problems with other people.

When those "what if…" thoughts come into my head, I just pray, "God, grant me the serenity…." If there is something I can change, I set forth to work out a plan for changing it, and the "it" most often is "I." Praying this prayer from the heart has helped me find serenity in every part of my life.

TODAY I WILL accept the things I cannot change and change the things I can.

July 12

Worry

One couple in our Families Anonymous group has had a rougher time than all the rest of us put together. Their child carries a dual diagnosis of personality disorder *and* chemical dependency. He has been in treatment half a dozen times, attempted suicide more than once, run away repeatedly, and spent time both in jail and in a locked psychiatric ward.

Throughout it all, they continued to come to meetings. Our hearts ached for them, and we wondered how they could endure. Finally, nearly bankrupt and stressed beyond belief, these two brave parents admitted their marriage had failed under the strain. We all felt their sadness.

Soon after their separation, a new member came to our group, describing the usual addiction agonies: "I can hardly stand this anxiety. It's driving me wild. Can you tell me what I must do?"

Our newly separated mom spoke up quietly. "Come back next week to FA, work the Steps, read the readings. Beyond that, remember one thing: *Worry is optional.*" It had cost her a great deal to learn that principle, but learn it she did.

TODAY I WILL choose to be at peace instead of tormenting myself with useless worry.

Wisdom

In the Serenity Prayer used in most Families Anonymous meetings, we ask for inner peace, for courage to do things that may be difficult or contrary to our own wills, and for discernment—the *wisdom to know the difference.*

Knowing the difference is rather like climbing a mountain. We start out loaded down with family obligations, the expectations and conventions of society, and our own prejudices and misconceptions. These burdens make it impossible for us to reach the mountain's peak—serenity.

Until we learn better, we enable rather than help. We judge and condemn rather than listen with an open mind. We vent our anger on unimportant issues. We are weighed down with guilt, blame, denial, fear, and despair. For a while, we continue to breathe the poisonous fumes of resentment, rejection, and regret. We are often in danger of losing our way, and some of us end up isolated and trapped.

But our climb becomes easier when we adopt the tools of the Twelve Step program. As we learn and grow, casting aside our unnecessary baggage, we find ourselves freer and climbing closer to the mountain's peak. Wisdom leads us to serenity.

TODAY I WILL seek the wisdom to know the difference.

July 14

Laughter

Chemical dependency is not an amusing subject. Yet our Families Anonymous meeting rooms often resound with the laughter of happy people. It's a mystery how we can be happy when we have all gone through our own private hells. How can we laugh? How can we *not* laugh?

Any newcomer can sense the joy of our program from the first smiles of welcome to the last cheerful goodbyes. We smile with relief and recognition as we speak about our own problems and listen as others share theirs.

Now we can laugh at situations that once brought us deep pain. An outsider might shake his or her head in astonishment as the group rocks with laughter, hearing a father explain the torturous way he tried to control his son, or a wife detailing her daily searches for evidence of a husband's using. Our own stupid, shameful actions don't seem so bad in this new and humorous light.

Before I found FA, my laughter was harsh and often cruel. Now I laugh with warmth and softness.

TODAY I WILL thank my Higher Power for this gift of joy, for laughter that enlivens my heart and heals my pain.

Control or Be Controlled?

It seems that things work best when they are under control. Water, under control, is a blessing. Fire, under control, is one of the most helpful elements. Many comforts seem to come from things under control. Most of us were taught, when young, that self-control is desirable. How, then, could control become such a terrible effort in dealing with people close to us who have the disease of chemical addiction?

For those of us living in the United States, our Constitution and Bill of Rights guarantee certain freedoms from outside controls. This is an ideal that people in many other nations also pursue. Outside control is something human beings do not tolerate easily. Yet some of us dare to try controlling the actions and lives of addicted persons!

Attempting to maintain control over such people requires tremendous energy. It takes time and attention. It deteriorates into preoccupation until we ourselves become obsessive and behave compulsively. Who, then, is in control? In trying to control, we become controlled by our own obsessions.

TODAY I WILL observe my tendency to control, then use it to control my own reactions, for the sake of my serenity.

July 16

Troubles

My grandmother knew a lot of sorrow during her long lifetime. In her old age, rather than grieving about the past and feeling sorry for herself, she found peace in acceptance. When another family member complained about some circumstance of life, she often asked, "If your troubles were in a bag with everyone else's, and you could reach inside and choose, wouldn't you settle for those you already have?"

Every time I start to feel sorry for myself, I remember Grandmother's Troubles Bag. Mentally I put my troubles into it along with the troubles of everyone else I can think of, and in the end I conclude I can handle my own better than any unfamiliar and perhaps worse ones.

Acceptance means cooperating humbly with whatever our Higher Power intends for us. I am grateful to God, for I know that every challenge of life contains an opportunity for me to grow. My Higher Power gives me the inner strength I need; I have but to believe in that strength and call upon it.

TODAY I WILL accept my challenges with courage and serenity.

Perspective

When I first came to Families Anonymous, I thought all I wanted from life was for my son to stop using drugs. Once he accepted help for his addiction and entered a treatment center, things got better. He became drug free, and our whole family began recovery. We all participated faithfully in support groups—our life lines.

But we still focused our hopes and dreams on the chemically dependent family member. Just as we had focused on his using, we now focused on his recovery. He stopped being our family scapegoat and became our family hero!

Recovery means much more than just getting the addict clean and sober. It means getting *all* our relationships back into the proper perspective. My husband and I need to work on our marriage, bruised and battered from years of neglect. Our nonaddicted children need to feel cared about and loved. All of us have to claim our own needs and feelings and move the former problem person out of the spotlight.

TODAY I WILL focus on my own recovery and allow others the same privilege.

July 18

Surrender

When my son was using drugs heavily, a constant prayer was on my lips and in my heart: "Oh God, please make him stop!" I said this prayer daily and nightly for years. Always religious, I couldn't understand God's apparent failure to intervene in my son's self-destruction. Finally, overwhelmed by despair, I gave up my prayer entirely.

That surrender marked the beginning of my own awakening. When I stopped giving orders to my Higher Power, I became open to God's will. When my meditation became silent rather than word-filled, I was ready for God's desires to be made known to me—not every day, and not always when I longed for answers, but without fail whenever God had a new message for me.

I began setting aside twenty minutes at the start of every day to open my heart to my Higher Power's direction. Faithfully honoring that daily quiet time was a challenge, but as I succeeded in doing so, my life soon began to change in many positive ways.

TODAY I WILL remember that in the stillness there is peace.

...Energy of My Own Personal Growth

Even though my son and other family members are in recovery, we still have our ups and downs; that's just life. We know disappointments. We have conflicts. We experience uncomfortable emotions and are still tempted to "stuff" them or escape them in some other way. In the old days, I let this emotional turmoil take its toll, until the physical consequences could no longer be ignored.

One of the solutions I found to support my recovery was walking for exercise. I started walking short distances and could barely make it. Then I got up to a mile. Now I can walk six miles and come home full of energy. Walking costs nothing, it is readily available, and the vitality it brings is a precious ingredient of my serenity.

When I slip into the old patterns and isolate myself, I have to struggle to take those first few steps out the door and down the street. Then as my muscles stretch out and my heart beats more strongly, my breathing deepens, my agitation lessens, and my interest in the beautiful world around me is renewed.

TODAY I WILL help my body recover its health.

July 20

Group Harmony

Participation in our Families Anonymous group has blessed me with caring friends. But this atmosphere of understanding and love became clouded when a parent joined our group whom I knew to have his own drug problem.

I squirmed at meetings as he "talked program" in what I thought was a self-deluded and superficial way. How did he expect his youngster to straighten up, when his own life was such a mess?

Others in the group sensed my disapproval and felt uncomfortable. This personality conflict was so powerful that I thought about dropping out of my beloved FA group. Talk about crazy thinking! What had happened to my recovery?

Thank goodness for our Steps and Traditions. With the help of other group members, I was able to take an inventory of *myself* rather than of this other person. I confessed my judgmental attitude and asked my Higher Power to remove it. I renewed my commitment to the Twelve Steps, let go of the other member and his problem, and stopped trying to control. The group's valuable unity was restored. Once again, the Twelve Steps and Twelve Traditions had shown me a better way to live.

TODAY I WILL judge only myself, and even then I will judge gently.

Growing in Gratitude

Looking at my gratitude list today, I recognize how much it has grown as I've grown in our fellowship. How did I ever overcome my anger, my guilt, and my compulsion to blame others while staying resentfully silent?

There are many Families Anonymous tools that have helped me along the way. Here are some of the things that I'm grateful for:

- FA's program, literature, and people
- on-the-job education and training derived from regular attendance at meetings
- a Higher Power that I can see at work in my life
- the new way of life that I practice daily in all my affairs
- the ability to take a good look at myself
- freedom from expectations, demands, control, useless anger, and blind reaction
- honesty and humility gained in our fellowship
- the person whose problems brought me to this program

I am grateful for *all* those things that have restored my ability to smile, laugh, and share in the fullness of life.

TODAY I WILL add something new to my gratitude list.

July 22

Blame

Society and some conventional "wisdom" would have us believe that our children's personalities are entirely the result of parental behavior and guidance. This mistaken idea places a great burden on parents. We worry and blame ourselves for every error and faltering step.

Thank goodness, this doesn't stand up to today's reality or the truths of the Twelve Step program. We do influence those we love, but we cannot play God in their lives. Our loved ones are free agents. Their personalities and unique characters are the result of many interactions of heredity, environment, and life experiences.

In Families Anonymous I've found that I will not always avoid mistakes or faulty decisions, but if I have tried hard and done my best in word and deed, loving without demand or obligation, blame is inappropriate. Our program teaches us not to be judgmental. With time and the FA program, I am able to accept the possibility of a mistake, admit it, learn from it, and leave it behind.

TODAY I WILL resist the tendency to blame myself and others. Instead, I will learn from my mistakes.

...In All My Affairs

The Families Anonymous program seems to work best for me when I use it willingly and consistently in my life. At first, I fell back on the program only when there was a crisis or problem involving a loved one. Eventually I discovered that applying the FA program selectively, to just one part of my life, set up a double standard. I was doing what I thought was necessary for my loved ones, but doing only what was *comfortable* in other areas of my life.

The Twelve Steps are meant to be used as a total program for life. When I distort the program to suit my own needs, all my progress seems to slip away, and I sacrifice everything I've accomplished. By taking only what I want to hear, I fall back into the old habits I've worked so hard to eradicate.

Life is more fulfilling for me when I remember a fundamental truth: the program works if I work it, every day, all the way. It is truly a blueprint for a serene life.

TODAY I WILL live the Twelve Steps and practice the FA program in all my affairs.

July 24

Meetings

I've heard that if I bring my body to meetings, my mind will eventually follow. And it's true that attending meetings permits me to experience, at first hand, the dynamics of people working together in their mutual quest for growth, understanding, and the peace of mind we call serenity.

But just attending meetings is not enough. There are no merit badges or gold stars for perfect attendance! It's important to come to a Families Anonymous meeting in a spirit of open-minded alertness, for when we do so, we discover great rewards.

There are no dues or fees, but there are some obligations. I am obligated to pay attention to the readings and give them more than lip service if I want to grow spiritually. I need to listen to others without wandering off into my own dreams and schemes, so that I can respond helpfully to their stories without passing judgment. And I must be truthful; dishonesty would be destructive to me as well as to the group.

TODAY I WILL give thanks for all the blessings I have received from Families Anonymous meetings.

Spiritual Awakening

The miraculous reward of working the Twelve Steps is the ability to face life squarely, without illusion or false optimism, and say, "It is good. It is very good!"

Staying in touch with one's Higher Power keeps alive this unconditional acceptance of life as it is.

As my awareness of my family's many problems increased, I was determined that I would do more than just survive. I believed that my Higher Power would see me through this painful time while I grew and changed. In spite of everything, I would thrive.

My thriving as a person is dependent not on outward circumstances but on a sense of identity with the fullness of life. Pain and disappointment are a part of that fullness, and so I ask for the grace to endure them without bitterness, in the joy of being alive and aware and free to grow.

The pain still hurts, but now I have perspective. Life is a mixture of sorrow and joy. I embrace it—overflowing with gratitude.

TODAY I WILL give thanks for the bounty of my life.

July 26

Daily Inventory

I once had a dream in which I kept storing things up in the attic until finally everything fell down on my head. As the parent of someone who misuses chemicals, I'm inclined to store up anger, hurt, resentment, and bad memories—none of which foster serene living.

Fortunately, the daily inventory of the Tenth Step keeps excess junk out of the "attic" of my life and on the "ground floor" of day-to-day reality, where I can handle it as it collects. How good it feels to recognize an old fault while its manifestation is still small and manageable, so that I can stop it dead in its tracks by admitting it!

The Tenth Step is also a humble reminder that I will never arrive at a final state of perfection. My inventory must be taken daily. Not only will I slip backward from time to time, but I am reminded that every achievement, no matter how hard won, can become an opportunity for false pride. Daily assessment keeps me on course.

TODAY I WILL let honesty, humility, and self-acceptance direct my actions and thoughts.

Action, Not Reaction

When my addicted son became sober, I was all too ready to step back into his life with a unique and complex system of punishments and rewards. As I bestowed blessings and reprisals, I was not acting but reacting. Such an approach on my part stunted my loved one's growth in his program.

Fortunately, I began attending Families Anonymous meetings and learned to act rather than react. I discovered that I can best demonstrate my love for my son by keeping out of his affairs. In fact, I need to stand back and let him hurt, fail, succeed, or get well without me there in the role of rescuing enabler. How much easier it is to do this when I use the tools of the program, practice the Twelve Steps, and focus on my own recovery.

TODAY I WILL *be* things for the person I am trying to help instead of doing things.

July 28

Letting Go

Every day I struggle with letting go. *Today* is a good day for me. *Today* I see that my child must make his way and solve his problems on his own. *Today* I understand that he will grow only as he himself sees and confronts his problems.

He and I are separate people. He must care for himself. I must take care of myself and my own needs, wants, and fears. I will not solve his problems for him, for if I do, I will keep both of us from growing into independent people.

Today I concentrate on my own growth. For many years I took care of my child's needs. Now I will take care of my own.

TODAY I WILL let go and let God.

Peacefulness

Peace comes from within. Strength replaces fear. The calm soothes my body. Where did it come from? Are there always answers? Are answers always necessary? Why not let some things remain a mystery?

I am thankful for the peace and strength I have found in the program of Families Anonymous. I treasure the feelings. Many things please me these days: geese flying overhead, a good book read by the fire, a phone call from a friend.

My life, strength, and sense of peace are miracles. I want to share this joy with others.

TODAY I WILL treasure the peacefulness I have earned.

July 30

Changing

Today I need some strength. Cold fingers of fear invade my chest, clutch at my heart. Where is my son? Why doesn't he see what he's doing to himself?

I pray for help so these chilling hurts will leave me. I pray for help to let go and let my Higher Power run things. I pray to remember all the changes I've made in my life since coming to Families Anonymous.

No longer willing to follow the old worrisome ways, I know that I need not submit to panic. Instead, I call an FA friend, read some comforting words in my FA literature, or focus on changing myself and my attitudes. I am thankful for all of these healthy changes in my life.

TODAY I WILL find strength in the progress I have made.

Things I Cannot Change

One thing I can never change is the past. When I'm inclined to fret about it, I remind myself that I did my job as well as possible. I was not perfect; no one is.

Doing the best I could do was *all* I could do. I did not cause my loved one's illness, so I will not reproach myself for what I might have done or said differently. This too is part of a past I cannot change.

I cannot make my child's disease go away, no matter how much I may wish that it would. I can only love him and love myself as well.

But there are two things I *can* change. One is my attitude. I can learn to detach with love, to let go and let God. I can release the past and its regrets in order to claim the treasures of today.

The other thing I can change is the expressions of my compassion. I can see my child as someone who hurts, who needs love, who will grow if he chooses to do so, *but only if I stand back and give him that opportunity.*

TODAY I WILL accept what I cannot change—and change what I can.

August 1

Step Five

Admitted to God, to ourselves, and to another human being the exact nature of our wrongs.

Step Five reminds me of the important risk I take when I reach out to others for acceptance, comfort, and understanding.

When I read my Fourth Step inventory to my sponsor, she helped me see that I was not as bad as I thought. She advised, "This is all in the past. You can throw away the parts that give you pain, and you can move on, knowing that you are forgiven as soon as you forgive yourself."

She helped me access my Higher Power. I realized that I had cut myself off from a valuable resource when I had failed to open up to others. An event or experience that seems overwhelming and unforgivable is brought down to size and made simpler when shared with another person.

I'll never forget how this same FA friend helped me sob openly during an especially painful period that called for yet another inventory followed by a Fifth Step. How healing those tears were! How comforting her words!

TODAY I WILL open up to another person as a Fifth Step way of reaching for my Higher Power.

Prescription

Someone in Families Anonymous said, "Wouldn't it be nice if there were a special medicine that would cure all the problems created by chemicals?"

There is such a medicine: the Twelve Steps of FA. But, as with all medicine, more than one dose is needed to cure our aches and pains. Our program, like life itself, is a continuing process. FA medicine is not always pleasant to take. It may be hard to swallow. It may make us feel strange. Old habits are hard to break.

But gradually, as we begin to feel better, we realize that the healthful program of FA is like vitamins: It benefits us most when we use it every day.

TODAY I WILL avail myself of FA's healing way.

August 3

To Sleep, Perchance…?

When I am troubled at night, and my mind is in turmoil because of some unsolved problem, I often lie awake, searching the darkness for some light or solution. Sleep escapes me; I feel that I must find the answer before I can rest.

Now I've learned to have a chat with my Higher Power at such times. I explain my dilemma, and together we come up with a solution. The most common solution is for me to go to sleep and hand over the problem to my Higher Power, knowing that it's in good hands.

And then I sleep in the knowledge that if it's right for me to have the answer, that answer will surface in the morning. If I don't get the answer, I will at least have the strength, after a good night's sleep, to cope with any and all eventualities that the day may bring.

TODAY I WILL turn over to my Higher Power any problem that's too big for me to solve alone.

Step Seven

Humbly asked him to remove our shortcomings.

After we *admitted to God, to ourselves, and to another human being the exact nature of our wrongs* in Step Five, we became willing and ready in Step Six to have these wrongs removed. Now, in Step Seven, we bring our acknowledged faults to the God of our understanding and humbly ask Him to remove those faults.

It's not as easy as it sounds, for over the years we've become attached to our various shortcomings, convinced that every one of them is justified!

By honestly and willingly working Step Seven and becoming free of old shortcomings, we find new and better ways of thinking and doing. We replace faults with good qualities, and we work toward getting comfortable with our true selves. With patience, we grow.

TODAY I WILL pray for the humility to recognize and relinquish the faults that have hindered my growth.

August 5

Reassurance

A little girl was awakened in the night by terrifying sounds—a thunderstorm was raging outside. She cried out in her alarm, and her clergyman father soon came to her side. He dried her tears, clasped her in a comforting hug, and patted her back to reassure her that all was well.

"Don't worry, Honey," he soothed. "You know God is going to watch over us."

"But Daddy," she wailed, "I want somebody *with some skin on them!*"

We too know that God will watch over us, but sometimes we're just like that little girl, craving the reassuring presence of somebody "with some skin on them."

When all seems hopeless, that is the moment to turn to a Families Anonymous friend. Dialing a telephone number and hearing a familiar voice is often all we need to make us feel better. An arm around our shoulder or a hug can give us the strength to go on.

Relying on a Higher Power is the FA way. So is letting a friend know you're having a rough day or being there yourself for someone else in trouble.

TODAY I WILL find reassurance in the love of God through my FA friends.

Attitude

I came to Families Anonymous hoping to find a way to help my drug-using family member. Instead, I discovered a lot about myself! The FA program helped me realize that I was sarcastic, suspicious, domineering, resentful, impatient, self-righteous, and judgmental. Learning this was very painful for me.

I tried to work on these defects of character. I tried a new way to live. I could cry, make mistakes, and admit when I was wrong. I learned to keep life simple and not expect so much of others.

One difficult thing I had to learn was *when to keep quiet.* As my son recovered, he was often hurting and depressed. He didn't need sarcasm; he needed love.

In a crisis, I tried to react intelligently rather than emotionally. Now when I start to fall back into my old ways, I read some FA literature and turn to my Higher Power until I am calm enough to deal with the situation I face.

My change of attitude has improved the atmosphere in our home and helps my son in his recovery.

TODAY I WILL cultivate an attitude that gives others the freedom to grow.

August 7

The Process of Change

I had been trying to follow the Twelve Steps for a long time before the meaning of Steps Six and Seven became clear. I was so hung up on control that I found it hard to see that these two Steps do not rely entirely on my will. It is my Higher Power, not I, that is in charge of my timetable for growth. My readiness and ability to change are not matters of conscious choice, but matters of grace.

I *became ready* to turn my will and my life over to that Higher Power, willing to risk trying something new. And then I *waited*—patiently or impatiently. But, as I have learned, wait I must.

Sometimes it seems that my Higher Power teaches me humility and surrender by making me wait longer than I think necessary to reach my goals. Yet who can say how long is necessary? It is not *my* goal for myself that matters, but God's will for my life.

When I am ready, I know it, because change comes effortlessly. What a relief! I no longer have to grit my teeth in grim determination.

TODAY I WILL trust my Higher Power to know what's next in my spiritual journey.

New Patterns

At times, as I work the Twelve Steps, I think I bog down between Steps Four and Nine in what seems like infuriating repetitiveness. The subtle progressions between each Step are difficult to see. But I need time to admit my inadequacies, to find new ways of living.

What makes it so hard for us to admit our shortcomings? One way of looking at shortcomings is as behavior patterns that used to work but now hamper growth. Many of the qualities we once prized as strengths became counterproductive when misused. We may follow old ways of controlling others and avoiding acceptance of responsibility for ourselves.

We can't begin to look for better ways of living until we recognize the ineffectiveness of the old ways and are ready to change. We need to practice these new ways before the actual removal of our shortcomings can come about through Step Seven.

TODAY I WILL live some of my new patterns with confidence and hope.

August 9

Changing Me

What is my true reason for following the Twelve Step way of life? Originally, it was the hope that I could cause a change in another. But Families Anonymous showed me that even if *I* changed for the better, the person whose problem led me to FA might choose not to change.

Through FA, I came to realize that my only responsibility is for myself. That is enough responsibility for a lifetime! I must want a better life for my own sake. Of course, I hope the changes I make will benefit those around me, but the outcome rests with my Higher Power.

Changing for the sake of influencing others is manipulative, self-defeating, and an obstacle to spiritual growth. My Higher Power will not support my delusions of grandeur, need for control, or self-glorification. Nowhere in the FA program does it say, "Follow the Twelve Steps and control the world."

TODAY I WILL rely on the Twelve Step way to become a better me.

Anger

Many of us were taught that anger is unacceptable, so we learned to deny this basic human emotion. We "stuffed it," blamed others, sulked, used the silent treatment, or overreacted instead. As a result, we hurt and alienated those around us.

Some of us learned to use anger to cover up other feelings, such as hurt, fear, and disappointment. By substituting anger for an honest expression of these emotions, we conceal our vulnerability and lack of control from those who are important to us.

Inappropriately expressed and uncontrolled anger can lead to physical abuse, family division, stress, illness, depression, irrational behavior, and loss of self-respect.

We begin to deal constructively with anger by acknowledging it. With effort, we may be able to detect the pattern in our responses that will help us deal with our anger appropriately and avoid being controlled by it. Just telling another caring person is a good way to begin.

Some constructive ways to deal with anger are to use a punching bag, talk it out with the right person, go for a walk, play a musical instrument with vigor, write a letter and don't mail it, or turn it over to a Higher Power.

TODAY I WILL accept my anger as a reality and channel it constructively.

August 11

Fear to Faith

Whenever I imagine that my children need the help that only I can give to save them from an unfortunate situation, I have to stop. I stop everything I am planning; stop any action I'm about to propose; stop thinking of alternatives that might work; and stop trying to fix everything.

I have to break away from the whirlpool that's waiting to suck me down—the whirlpool of irrationality that immerses me so completely in another's problems that I no longer exist for myself.

I remind myself of past occasions when I permitted my children to work out their own solutions—and how well they did without my interference.

Sometimes it is only fear that spurs me to action: fear that without my help they will be incapable of solving their problems, fear that they will make things even worse, fear that they may ruin their lives, *fear that they no longer need me!*

When I allow fear and insecurity to dominate my thinking, I become an obstacle to my own growth and to the growth of my children. My Higher Power really does guide others as well as me.

TODAY I WILL overcome fear with faith.

Forgiveness

Too often, the notion of forgiveness is overlooked, as if it were merely some sort of unrealistic religious concept. In fact, forgiveness is the spiritual foundation of letting go, of self-esteem, and of serenity and recovery.

An interesting attribute of forgiveness is that it proceeds from inside out. We get angry about those characteristics in others that we most dislike in ourselves. So we must forgive ourselves before we can forgive others.

The act of forgiving ourselves makes it possible to let go of the drug user by forgiving him or her. It allows us to regain our self-esteem by refocusing our energy away from the abuser and onto ourselves. Self-forgiveness lifts the heavy burden of guilt, anger, resentment, and hate so that we can achieve serenity.

As one of the spiritual foundations of recovery, forgiveness is a good daily ritual when it is focused properly on oneself. Then forgiveness of others can follow. This focus helps in my recovery and in the recovery of others.

TODAY I WILL forgive my own shortcomings so that I can then forgive the shortcomings of others.

August 13

I Have a Choice

I have received a gift from my friends in Families Anonymous. It's four little words: "I have a choice." I've made little posters of these words and taped them to my bathroom mirror and across my office desk.

What do these words mean to me? They remind me that I do, indeed, have a choice about many things. I can ride on "automatic pilot" and follow my lifelong habit of reacting rather than acting, or I can choose to follow the FA program and act in responsible ways. I can stop altering my life to suit the demands of others. I can give up enabling the destructive behavior of a loved one. I can say what I mean, mean what I say, and recover my own dignity.

With four little words posted here and there in my environment, I'm finding it progressively easier to make choices that assist my recovery and to let go of an obsessive lifestyle that offers no choices.

TODAY I WILL look forward to this new day and new chance to make my own choices.

An Affirmation

"The spirit of God is within me. The grace of God surrounds me." This is an affirmation I repeat many times when I am in special need of a spiritual lift. In the midst of turmoil, or as I tremble my way through a rough time, I may find it necessary to say these words over and over.

At less stressful times, I'm often helped by getting up early in the morning, sitting quietly, and inhaling the fresh morning air as I visualize the light of this spirit and this grace coming into me. Then as I exhale, I try to feel the grace flowing out and around me, filling my world.

TODAY I WILL take time to affirm a close tie with a Higher Power.

August 15

Meetings—the Twelfth Step

Many times someone has said to me, "Your addict doesn't live with you any longer. Why do you still attend those Families Anonymous meetings?"

It's not hard for me to remember why. When I walked into my first FA meeting, I felt helpless and totally alone. When the meeting ended, I realized that I could not control my addict—but that I needed to learn to control my emotions in order to cope with everyday problems.

As I became more involved in the program, I learned that I was not alone. So many of the stories being shared were the same. Only the names were different.

Who would have been there for me if everyone whose addict was in recovery or had left home stopped attending meetings? Someone was there when I was in need. I will be there when someone else needs the group.

TODAY I WILL be ready to pass on the help and hope that was given to me when I was a newcomer.

Living Today

When we first come to a Families Anonymous meeting, we are filled with many negative emotions: frustration, anger, worry, guilt.

More often than not, we are focused on the past. "Why did this happen to me?"

We worry about the future. "What's going to happen to us?"

We berate ourselves for our helplessness in this problem. Yet such reactions deplete our energies.

In FA, we learn a new way of life, one that puts us on the path to serenity. We learn to let go of the past and stop worrying about the future. Our task is to deal with the present—today. We concentrate on *what is* instead of *what was* or *what will be.*

The past is gone, never to return again. Today is all we can be sure about. The future is not yet here, but what we do now *can* influence its outcome.

TODAY I WILL release the past and the future, knowing that *living today is the only way to have a life.*

August 17

Release with Love

My years of child rearing have provided me with plenty of practice in releasing with love. I remember how difficult it was for me to turn my child over to a babysitter. I recall how many times I had to let him fall down as he learned to walk. The decision to remove training wheels from his bicycle was traumatic. Allowing him to walk to school alone was a challenge for both of us. I watched his first jump from a diving board with a mixture of fear and pride.

As he grew older, I had to let him fail and go to summer school to make up his grades. Without my reminders, he forgot to mow the neighbor's lawn and lost the job.

Now, as the parent of an older adolescent, I have to continue releasing with love. This means locking the door when he's late. It means not paying his court fines. It means stepping back and allowing him the dignity of using his own money to fix the car he damaged.

TODAY I WILL release my child with love in order that both of us may grow and know the satisfaction of mature independence.

Detach with Love

Detaching from my loved one's problems was probably the most difficult thing I ever had to do. Through the Families Anonymous program, I gained strength to take the necessary actions to extricate myself from the family disease of chemical dependency. At the same time, I became able to allow my loved one the dignity to learn and grow by experiencing both successes and failures. I found the words that help me communicate love while declaring my detachment.

As I changed and progressed, I was better prepared for those times when my addicted son called to ask for money or something else that would enable him to continue using drugs.

"I love you," I told him, "but I can't help you. You know where to get help. I'm sure you'll work out your problems and make the right choices." I've had an opportunity to make this statement a number of times.

If I were to do otherwise, I would be saying, in effect, "You're too weak to grow and take care of yourself." When I say the words now that demonstrate my loving detachment, I further my own recovery and avoid standing in the way of his.

TODAY I WILL detach with love, in thought, word, and deed.

August 19

Simple Words

"God be with me. Thy will be done." Even as a young child, I found comfort in these simple words. Today I call this my "fear prayer." When I am overcome with rational or irrational dread, I repeat this prayer quietly or within my thoughts.

This little prayer keeps me from sinking into frozen fear and allows me to function and go on with life. Through its strength, I am able to do what needs to be done. Through it, I'm also able to convey some sense of stability to others who may be prone to panic.

TODAY I WILL rely on simple, surrendered prayer and the strengths of the Families Anonymous program.

Tradition Twelve

Anonymity is the spiritual foundation of our program, ever reminding us to place principles above personalities.

So states the Twelfth Tradition of Families Anonymous. It means that I can share my feelings and experiences without fear that anyone will carry them beyond the walls of my FA meeting room. It also means that I hold in trust any confidences revealed during a meeting or in private conversation with another FA member. This is how I can feel secure in relieving my burdened heart.

Another way of expressing this cherished tradition goes like this:

Whom you see here,
What we say here,
When you leave here,
Let it stay here.

TODAY I WILL trust others with my story while I guard theirs with care.

August 21

Inventory

Guilt—appropriate or inappropriate—is one of the most painful and destructive emotions confronting the family of an addicted person. My guilt made me almost eager to begin Step Four. I thought, "I'll admit to anything—even to being Jack the Ripper—if it will help my loved one."

Such misplaced guilt is really arrogance. It implies, "I am so important that anything that goes wrong must be my fault. If I can just figure out what I've done wrong, I can fix the imperfection and make everything all right again."

In reality, no one has that much power. We delude ourselves by thinking that we do. However, I *am* responsible for my own actions.

I do often respond in ways that are less than helpful. Accepting guilt for everything that goes wrong is one of those ways.

TODAY I WILL use my inventory to shape a realistic sense of responsibility.

Step Eight

For me, giving up resentment is what Step Eight is all about. Holding onto resentment is perhaps the most common way family members harm each other and those outside the family.

During the denial stage of this family illness, concerned friends and family are often as paranoid as the drug user. I cringe when I think of the resentment I harbored toward those who tried to help me face the truth. Those friends go on my list of persons I have harmed.

Other family members also go on my list—those who suffered blame, neglect, and my martyrdom as I struggled to cope alone, shutting them off from what should have been a family effort.

I harmed the drug user in my household when I failed to fully accept and understand the true nature of her illness. Although she appeared to be living life as one great big party, I failed to appreciate the fear, guilt, and self-hatred she must have felt. And I blamed her for not asking for help before she was ready.

But I am the person I harmed most of all. I need inner harmony too much to let harsh judgments and self-justification divide me against myself.

TODAY I WILL give up resentments.

August 23

Making Amends

Dear Inner Self,

I'm writing you in a sincere effort to make amends. I'm sorry for all the hell I've put you through. I kept you from getting the help you needed. I made impossible demands on you, then punished you when you couldn't live up to those unrealistic expectations.

I underestimated your capacity to take full responsibility for your life. I doubted you when you forced me to fully experience my painful emotions. I accused you of trying to drive me crazy when you were really trying to drive me sane. I downplayed the times when you showed me genuine compassion and concern. I scoffed at your words of wisdom. You always possessed the courage and strength I needed, but I was too scared to trust you.

Now you are my best friend and good company when I'm frightened and alone. I need you, and you need me. You connect me to my Higher Power, and I connect you to the outer world. We make a great team. Thank you for staying with me even when I let you down.

Love,
Your Outer Self

TODAY I WILL make peace with myself as the way to be at peace with the world.

Giving Credit

A recent addition to popular vocabulary has been the term *dysfunctional family*. Numerous treatment professionals use it, as do many of us in Twelve Step programs. I often referred to my family as "dysfunctional," until my three adult children came home one Thanksgiving.

As I was expressing gratitude for the recovery of "our dysfunctional family," my oldest stopped me. "Wait a minute," he said. "I think we've called ourselves 'dysfunctional' long enough. Look at all the things we're doing well. I think we're pretty darn functional these days."

My daughter chimed in. "I agree! I'm tired of being labeled 'dysfunctional.' We all try constantly to improve communications, get along better, and be healthier and more whole. All of that seems extremely functional to me! How many other families put out this much effort in the interest of creating a better life?"

They were right. It was time to stop labeling ourselves and to give credit for the many things we do well. Old labels were standing in the way of our recovery.

TODAY I WILL give credit where credit is due—to my family, to others, and to myself.

August 25

Serenity

God, grant me the serenity to accept the things I cannot change....

Recently, that first line of the Serenity Prayer was the subject of our meeting. Several parents who had been attending meetings for only a few weeks spoke of the newfound sense of relief they experienced when they realized they could stop struggling over problems they couldn't control. They spoke of finding calm, even in crisis. This is serenity—a big step for beginners.

But not everyone "gets" the program right away. One persistent mother continued to interrupt again and again, describing the alcoholism of her daughter and her own determination to supervise and control the life of a woman 46 years old who had had four husbands! It will take time, but perhaps eventually she'll see what a useless struggle it is to try to control another person's life. As her serenity grows, she may even enjoy the luxury of being able to laugh at herself.

TODAY I WILL claim serenity, giving up the futile struggle for power over that which I cannot control.

Please, Just Listen

When I ask you to listen and you give me advice instead, you have not met my need.

When I ask you to listen and you tell me I shouldn't feel that way, you trample on my feelings.

When I ask you to listen and you offer solutions, you have failed me, strange as that may seem.

Listen! All I ask is that you listen, not tell me what to do.

I *can* do for myself. I'm not helpless—maybe discouraged and faltering, but not helpless. Your solution may be right for you; I must find the one that works for me. I can do this only by accepting my feelings as real, trying to discover what lies behind those feelings, and then calmly looking for the best solution.

I don't need advice. I do need you to reflect my feelings by listening, then helping me to see my own choices. And then I'll listen to you.

TODAY I WILL listen.

August 27

The Higher Power

The Families Anonymous concept of a Higher Power is challenging for me. No, I'm not an atheist. I don't spend much time thinking about whether or not there's a God. Agnostic? No, not really. I just have never developed a feeling about God, one way or the other. And I suspect I'm far from being alone in what many describe as an increasingly secular society.

After my wife and I discovered our 16-year-old was an addict and an alcoholic, we were introduced to a series of spiritual concepts. While our boy was in the hospital, we attended many therapy sessions, all ending with the Serenity Prayer.

After our child was released from treatment, we joined Families Anonymous, where we were introduced to the famous Twelve Steps. Today, I still have much to learn. For the present, my Higher Power is the FA group itself.

Strange? A cop-out? Denial? In many self-help groups, secular types like me find that a good place to start is by letting the group be our Higher Power. For here in these groups are many who are devout and many, like me, who are still in doubt—but growing.

TODAY I WILL draw on a Higher Power by being humble enough to ask for guidance and inspiration.

Don't *E*ase *G*od *O*ut

After conscientiously working the program of Families Anonymous for many years, I find my many defects are becoming apparent. And, oh so slowly, my attempts to change these defects are beginning to have results.

The Eleventh Step reminds me to never be complacent—to never be so proud of my growth that I forget that nothing could ever be achieved without my Higher Power. To let my *ego* get in the way is to *E*ase *G*od *O*ut—to say, "I don't need You every day, God. I can do it without You." *Wrong!*

When I *E*ase *G*od *O*ut, I rob myself of the quiet time that can come each day to bring me peace and serenity.

*E*asing *G*od *O*ut pulls me away from the core of my spiritual center and causes me to forget, "Your will be done." It diminishes the goodness in me and causes me to forget the source of my serenity.

TODAY I WILL pray, "Be with me. I need You."

August 29

Working Through the Pain

It's hard to accept the pain of a loved one's dependence on chemicals. It takes courage to acknowledge and live through the heartache, hurt, and fear. And who, in his or her right mind, seeks out pain?

Maybe I wasn't in my right mind for a long time, even after I joined Families Anonymous. I was one of the lucky ones. My son chose to go into treatment. I was eager to see my child grow in the program. Even though we had many setbacks, I always looked on the bright side. Even when my son decided to use again, I refused to be upset. I relied on the support and love of my FA group and wouldn't let his choice get *me* down.

It took my son's attempted suicide to slam me up against reality. For once, my happy-go-lucky attitude couldn't carry me through. I felt real pain, and it hurt!

Slowly I began to realize how foolish I'd been. I had seen the silver lining, but not the cloud; I had seen the light, but never the tunnel. My own lack of maturity had kept me from growing, for there is no growth without *pain*. My fears had kept me from healing, for there is no recovery without living through the *pain*. My blindness had kept me from fully helping others, for there is no empathy without experiencing *pain*.

TODAY I WILL not avoid *pain* but will accept it as part of my healing process.

Step Ten

Continued to take personal inventory, and when we were wrong, promptly admitted it.

Since I've been attending Families Anonymous meetings, I've learned that each Step requires a careful reading, with attention to every word. In Step Ten, the word *continued* reminds me that this is a Step I need to take on a continual, daily basis.

The word *personal* means that I am the only person I should be concerned with in this Step. This Step is my assessment of myself, not of anyone else.

An inventory is a list of what's in stock. At the end of each day, I can take a look at myself: what I've accomplished, mistakes I've made, and how I need to proceed. I ask myself, "Have I let a Higher Power lead and guide my life today, or have I tried to *be* a Higher Power?"

The second part of Step Ten tells me to admit my wrongs as soon as possible. I may admit them to myself, to God, and, if appropriate, to someone else. At this point, I can plan ways to correct my mistakes, if possible, and give myself credit for progress rather than perfection.

TODAY I WILL use my daily inventory to help me apply the Twelve Steps to my life.

August 31

Letting Go

What is *letting go*? It's a gift from our Higher Power, a gift so powerful that it can erase past hurts. It allows us to love freely and accept our children as they are.

It means no expectations—not even a birthday card. It means, "I love you, because you are a child of God and worthy of love." It means I will love today, no matter what is said or done. It means I will stop trying to control and will trust in a loving Higher Power. It means detaching from other people, places, and things in order to fulfill hopes and dreams of my own.

Letting go means getting started!

Letting go is a lifetime project. We never graduate with honors. Some days we achieve a good grade, some days not so good, but we keep trying. Every glimmer of growth makes it worth the struggle.

Letting go means giving my loved one the dignity to lead his own life.

As I grow in my ability to let go, I can begin to learn about me and see the beauty within me. My crisis times were stormy and troubled, and I did whatever I could to survive. Now, when I detach, I see the storm end and often find a beautiful rainbow—my serenity.

TODAY I WILL let go.

Let Go and Let God

What does *let go and let God* mean to each of us? Does it mean having faith and expecting guidance, or does it mean resignation and hopelessness? Does it mean abandoning a commitment to act on God's inspiration and guidance—in other words, expecting God to "do it all"?

Sometimes we work very hard to bring a difficult situation to a successful conclusion—yet the desired outcome still eludes us. At that point, the best solution, the only *real* solution, is to *let go and let God.*

The simple act of releasing our needs to a Higher Power is not one of abandoning our responsibility, but rather one of opening the door to any God-given possibility. Divine power can deal with matters that are beyond us. When we finally trust our Higher Power for help, we see things happen that we could never bring to pass on our own. Perhaps this will convince us that another person's actions and fate are not in our hands.

TODAY I WILL sing to myself, "He's got the whole world in His hands...."

September 2

Fear

> All fear is a sign of want of faith.
> –Mohandas Gandhi

When I find myself falling into the old pattern of trying to control or manipulate, I remember the self-service car wash. All I do is put in my money and stay in the car, position the front wheels, shift into neutral, and let go of the steering wheel.

Even though it's a little scary in there with the water beating down and those huge brushes whirling against the car, I know it would be disastrous to try to steer. For a short time, I am truly powerless. All I can do is surrender and trust that I will come out all in one piece, clean and shiny.

Surrender to the program is much the same. Once my feet have been firmly placed on the correct path, I can follow the Twelve Steps, serene in the knowledge that many others have gone before me and have, indeed, emerged refreshed and whole.

TODAY I WILL let go of the "steering wheel" and trust in the program, drawing strength from my Higher Power and from those who have gone before me.

Service

Joining is something I used to avoid. Whenever I joined a church or other organization, I was asked to contribute money or time. I just wanted to go there, get the message, and go home. I didn't want to take time for meetings and such.

When I began to have problems at home, I showed up at some Families Anonymous meetings—reluctantly. Sometimes I even got there in time for the opening readings.

I started to feel a bit better about my home situation. Then I heard that service was part of my recovery. "There it is again," I thought. "They want my time."

In an FA meeting, someone said, "I wish I had back all the hours I've spent worrying about this problem when I could have been enjoying life."

I went home and estimated how many hours I had spent talking about our family problems to anyone who'd listen, how many days I had sat idle, isolated with my misery. I thought, "How much time would it take to be the group secretary?" Probably only a few hours a week—getting there a little early to set up and start the coffee, a little bit more to keep track of the money and literature. It added up to far fewer hours than I'd been squandering on worry.

I volunteered to be secretary for our group, and I continue to give service where I can. Service has paid off in quality recovery.

TODAY I WILL give service for the good of the group, for the total organization of FA, and most of all for myself.

September 4

Honesty

Attending Families Anonymous meetings is usually comfortable and comforting. But sometimes in a meeting we are led to confront ourselves. We may come face to face with problems we have not acknowledged. If dishonesty or denial makes us unwilling to admit our fears, we cannot solve our problems.

Whether we realize it or not, we always have a choice. We can maintain our established ways or try new and more courageous ones. A decision may be forced upon us when we suddenly see our own faults in another person. Soon we gain new insights into our own behavior.

Working the Twelve Steps requires honesty. Once a fault has become a way of life, we can correct it only if we truly desire to change. Will my Higher Power give my friends the courage to speak up and help me gain insight? Will my Higher Power give me the courage to correct my faults?

TODAY I WILL shine the light of honesty behind any "curtains" I may have drawn over my guilts, fears, and angers.

Character Defects

I was overwhelmed after my first Families Anonymous meeting. I liked what I heard, but I also realized that I had a lifetime of habits to change.

My pattern had always been to improve upon family members' ideas and plans. I could see the pitfalls in some of their decisions, and I wanted to protect them.

Now it was clear that I needed to back off, get out of the way, and allow the people I care about to direct their own lives.

I had to stop thinking for everyone else in the family. No longer could I tell my spouse what to do. My teenage children were certainly bright enough to take care of themselves. The Manager Me had to resign.

Along the way, everyone in my household has suffered some painful consequences, but many of the choices made by others have turned out to be better than mine.

I'm now ready to have God remove my annoying character defects, especially those that block someone else's personal growth.

TODAY I WILL relinquish my need to control.

September 6

Attitudes

I want to feel better inside. I want more serenity instead of the uneasy feeling I've had for so long. Families Anonymous has shown me that I can feel better if I change the way I look at things.

Clinging to negative thoughts holds me back and keeps me from solving my problems and getting on with my life. I can decide to put my negative thoughts aside and replace them with positive ones.

Every situation, no matter how unpleasant or frightening, contains something good. That "something" may be simply a challenge for me to grow, which in itself is a very valuable experience.

If I develop an attitude of looking for the good in all things, I will be able to see the beauty in the world, and my life will be enriched. If I pay attention to the visual feast of autumn, the welcome hush when a blanket of new snow has fallen, the first bite of an apple, the music of a child's laugh, and the many other wonders in life, they will bring me much joy.

I *can* do this if I really want to, going ahead one day at a time. I *can* live in the moment and make the most of the good things all around me.

TODAY I WILL find something to admire and enjoy.

That First Step Again

After studying Steps One through Twelve, our Families Anonymous group started on Step One again. As always, we found something new in it.

One of the most perceptive observations was shared by a longtime member. We had been discussing the meaning of *powerlessness* and *letting go* when she came up with this profound statement: "Whatever it is, it is *not* rejection."

When others who misuse drugs have difficulty recognizing the fact that they need help, we look for ways to help. Certainly, rejecting them is not helpful. Being soft on them is not an option either. There's a world of difference between being firm with our loved ones and turning our backs on them.

Perhaps the most persuasive argument against seeing *letting go* as rejection is that *letting go* improves our chances to be of real help when our loved one finally recognizes the problem and seeks recovery.

TODAY I WILL refuse to care *for* my addict while remaining willing to care *about* him.

September 8

Step Six

Were entirely ready to have God remove all these defects of character.

In taking Steps Four and Five, I explored and found some of my character defects. Now, if I really want to cure my defects, I need to be *entirely ready*.

Letting go of faults is difficult because they have been a part of me for so long. Some of these traits are almost instinctive reactions.

In some cases, I will need a new way of thinking in order to change. Take honesty, for instance. In an effort to be a nice guy, at times I have said and done things just to please others, knowing I was being dishonest.

I also know that I am often still anxious, wanting to control others rather than allowing them to choose their own actions. We know our addicts must take the consequences for their mistakes; now I find I must put this knowledge into practice. This is a positive move for me. I'm beginning to practice what I preach.

Admitting my defects and being ready for change, with the help of my Higher Power, has made a difference. My part is to be conscious of my faults and be ready to have them removed.

TODAY I WILL change, with God's help. I need not continue making the same mistakes.

Humility

Our whole society is geared toward material success and pride in achievements. We want success for ourselves and our children. Failure is the last thing we seek.

Most of us view humility as a useful safeguard against conceit. Some wise person observed that humility comes only through failure. We who have come to Families Anonymous have known profound feelings of failure and defeat.

When we heard Step Seven being discussed, we began to learn that these same feelings of failure could work to our advantage. They give us the humility needed to learn a new way of life: a life with peace of mind and contentment in spite of unsolved problems.

As long as we thought our self-reliance was our most valuable asset, we were kept from the only thing that could bring us peace of mind—a genuine reliance upon a Higher Power.

Failure can be an asset, if it gives us humility and a desire to seek and do God's will. Why waste our failures? We can use them to bring us closer to God's will for us: joy, peace, and serenity.

TODAY I WILL be humbly grateful for the failures that make me ready for a new way of life.

September 10

Taking Care of Me

It looks as though my drug-using child will never give up his self-destructive ways. But, strange as it may seem to those unfamiliar with Families Anonymous and its program, I'm really a happier person today. I used to make a career of worrying about what other people were doing or not doing. Now I've learned to stop managing other people's lives and to take care of myself. I'm doing something I've always wanted to do but have never felt I could spend the time, effort, and money on: learning to sail.

Now I feel young and healthy again, and this creates a better atmosphere in my home. When my son visits, he can feel the difference. If he ever does get into recovery, he will have a healthier, happier parent.

Whatever led me to Families Anonymous, I'm grateful to the program for giving me back to myself.

TODAY I WILL take care of myself. I deserve it!

Obsession

I attended many Families Anonymous meetings before I could admit that my own obsession with other people and their problems was every bit as compelling as an addiction to drugs or alcohol. I worried about each member of my family. I wanted to change them, guide them, lead them in the "right" direction.

I went even further in my obsession. I took on the cares and woes of everyone—my fellow workers, the grocery checker, even other patients in my doctor's waiting room.

Why did I assign myself the role of *The Great Rescuer?* A bit of therapy and some new knowledge about codependency helped me understand my addiction to other people's problems.

Through study of the Twelve Step program, I am learning to deal with my obsession. I write down things I'm obsessed with, and then I place the paper in a receptacle that I call my "God Box." I'm still hoping to get rid of my obsessive habit once and for all, but for the present, in my daily meditation, I give it to a Higher Power.

As I give my obsession away, one day at a time, in the same way an alcoholic gives up his wish to drink, I remind myself that, just for today, I am free of my obsession. I'm no longer in possession of it today, nor is it in possession of me. This helps me resist the temptation to rescue or try to change others.

TODAY I WILL turn over my obsession to my Higher Power and be ready to do so again tomorrow.

September 12

What's Important?

A friend's 20-year-old was wandering all over the country, following a band whose concerts are notorious for audience drug use. My family's concern for this boy was great, knowing he was sliding downhill, using chemicals that might destroy him forever.

I invited the mother and father to Families Anonymous, telling them it was a fellowship where those with similar experiences could offer encouragement and support. But the proud and grieving parents preferred to nurse their pain in isolation. I still hoped they would change their minds.

"What he's doing may kill him," I said. "Would you come if the knowledge you gained could save his life?"

"Oh, we're not worried about his life," the mother replied. "We just wish he'd get a haircut!"

An FA slogan asks a critical question: *How important is it?* A haircut is not very important. Addiction is all-important—a matter of life or death. I ask myself this question many times in the course of a week, and the answers always guide me in making my choices wise ones.

TODAY I WILL ask, "How important is it?" Then I will act accordingly.

Grieve, Then Grow

The pain, tears, and mourning experienced because of a beloved addict often seem more than one can bear. It's like facing a death, yet not so final. In the case of the addict, we experience that pain again and again, each time a possible recovery turns into another downfall.

But Families Anonymous teaches hope through growth. Tapping into our Higher Power helps us begin to ease the grief. Miraculously, we start to build a new way of life that brings countless dividends. We learn that emotional growth takes time for those who suffer with the family disease of addiction. Moving beyond our suffering, lovingly supported by our FA friends, we gradually become less judgmental of others, more accepting, closer to our fellow human beings. We develop a deeper humility and gratitude.

Eventually, we rediscover joys in life we never expected to know again. Sometimes we experience these joys, amazingly enough, in spite of a continuing unsolved problem.

TODAY I WILL work my program patiently, confident that someday my sorrow may turn to joy.

September 14

Keep It Simple

Each person in a Families Anonymous group wrote a short statement about the slogan, *Keep it simple.*

Keep it simple means easing myself into a spiritual wavelength of surrender, taking no immediate action except to *let go and let God.*

When *one day at a time* is too much for me, I *keep it simple* by living one moment at a time.

I *keep it simple* by emptying my head of complicated thoughts and, instead, truly accepting what I can or cannot change.

*Keeping it simpl*e helps me remember whose problem is whose, and it helps me to focus on myself—on what I can do for me.

I can *keep it simple* by praying only for knowledge of my Higher Power's will for me and for strength to carry out that will.

Keep it simple! I can stop being so compulsive and remind myself I don't have to accomplish everything all at once. I can let go and take time to enjoy life's gifts, one day at a time.

Keep it simple means neither looking back nor burdening myself with expectations beyond my own abilities or the abilities of another.

TODAY I WILL keep it simple.

Faith

In the Families Anonymous program, I have learned that I do not have complete control over my life and the lives of others and that I cannot rely solely on my own power. If I am to find lasting peace and tranquility, I must surrender to my Higher Power and accept that God can do a much better job of running things than I can. I came to this program out of desperation after all of my attempts to exercise control had failed. Now I have become willing to go to any length to achieve and maintain serenity.

Faith the size of a mustard seed is all I need to work the program. I must nourish this seed, lest it fall by the wayside. I learn to replace fear with faith and decide to act *in spite of* fear, not *because* of it. This is a daily task, a lifelong process. Once I have sincerely and honestly made this decision and acted upon it, my life will begin to change. This is the hope our program offers.

TODAY I WILL call upon faith to help me replace my willfulness with willingness, relying on my Higher Power for direction.

September 16

Humor

I often hear others say at meetings how good it is to be able to laugh again. I agree! There are many kinds of laughter. One particular kind arises from a sense of relief. Perhaps this is what first brings laughter back to our lives.

Humor keeps me on a steady and pleasant emotional course day-by-day. It helps me avoid the extremes of misdirected anger or silent self-torment.

With humor, I can break through the facade of fear and fury, leaving my old grouchy, ill-humored self behind. With humor, I can seek the good in any situation, keeping my wits about me and my spirits high. Humor helps me see myself in an honest and natural way.

In the Families Anonymous program, I've learned to use humor rather than anger to tell someone how I feel and to remain pleasant even when I feel rejected, put down, or hurt.

Humor is rooted in humanity and humility. Good humor means smiling, exchanging jokes, and refusing to laugh at the expense of another. It is a good tool for living a useful and purposeful life, even in the presence of unsolved problems. Humor is one of life's special gifts, healing and restorative.

TODAY I WILL find something to laugh at, knowing there is more to be gained from a smile than a frown.

Seeds of Recovery

At one stage in my recovery, I realized that I was slipping backwards. I had fallen into that old trap of thinking that all the knowledge I had accumulated would help my recovery. I had forgotten that knowledge *without action* is of no use whatsoever. Even though I attended Families Anonymous meetings and thought I was working my program, I was only "talking it," not "walking it." A fellow FA member helped me with this observation:

"It's as if you once sowed a seed, and as a plant grew from that seed, you looked after it, nurtured it, and cared for it until it blossomed. But after that, you neglected the plant, and it 'went to seed.'"

She needed to say no more. I hadn't been putting the same loving care into collecting and planting and nurturing new seeds, so of course they weren't growing as well as the first one had.

I am grateful for my friend's analogy. I need constant reminders that ours is a daily program. The work of recovery requires constant attention. It's as if our program is an annual plant, not the hardy perennial for which I'd mistaken it.

TODAY I WILL remember that the FA program is a pattern of living that works if I work it.

September 18

Frustration

The only way I can continue living comfortably with the knowledge that a loved one is chemically dependent is to deal with one problem or frustration at a time.

In the past, I responded to each new crisis in my life by mentally enumerating and reliving all my previous misfortunes. The result was a feeling of being totally overwhelmed by negativity. Since I've changed this pattern, I feel much calmer and better equipped to face whatever comes.

Today, whenever I encounter someone at a Families Anonymous meeting or another friend who's going through a stressful time, I try to be especially patient, tolerant, and supportive. Many times in the past, I took my frustration out on an innocent person when I was at the end of my rope with my own family problems.

If I dwell on the crises I've been through, the result is self-pity; but if I take other people's stresses and hardships into account, I can be more compassionate.

TODAY I WILL ration myself to dealing with one immediate problem at a time.

Unexpected Education

Through Families Anonymous, I've received an unexpected education about myself. What have I learned, and what is the result?

I have learned…

- that there is nothing I can do to change my son. I have given up worrying.
- to let my son be responsible for his own actions. I have laid aside a burden.
- that I am important and deserve a happy life. I have let go of anger.
- to stop lecturing, plotting, rescuing, and nagging. I have lessened my frustration.
- that my son's illness is not my fault. I have abandoned my guilt.
- to detach from my son's problem. I have gained a sense of freedom.
- that martyrs don't necessarily go to heaven. I have laid aside my victimhood.
- to look at my faults and my good qualities. I have started to grow.
- to set limits. I have gained structure in my life.
- to love my son unconditionally. I have stopped hating.
- to laugh again. I have rediscovered life's joys.

TODAY I WILL learn at least one new thing in the FA program.

September 20

Self-Pity

When doing for others, I often feel overwhelmed and drained. When others don't live up to my expectations, I feel disappointed and fall into the trap of anger, resentment, and self-pity. But the truth is that my anger is frequently directed at myself for allowing others to trigger these negative emotions in me.

One of my defects of character seems to be a tendency to do for others what they can do for themselves, even when they'd rather not accept my help. Then I feel sorry for myself. Am I part of the problem instead of part of the solution?

If I slip back into negative thinking, I become hard on myself. When I "work the program," on the other hand, I am good to myself. I don't expect perfection, and I accept my own and others' vulnerability.

Accepting others is much easier when I know and accept myself. I can stop being a martyr, recognize my limitations, and then go back to being a human being again.

TODAY I WILL stop feeling sorry for myself and grow in healthy new ways.

Patterns

I sometimes find myself stuck in a never-ending cycle of dealing with the problems of living. I deal with my life as I saw my parents deal with theirs, and my parents dealt with their lives as they had seen their own parents do.

Until I become willing to break out of the cycle and create a new pattern for my life, I remain stuck. Only by working the Families Anonymous program on a daily basis do I stand a chance of making the changes that can lead to a better way of life for my family and me. I am grateful that new ways of living can begin today, starting with me.

TODAY I WILL try a different way of dealing with life rather than blindly following the unhealthy patterns of the past.

September 22

Listening

Negative criticism is hard to take and easy to give. Other people rarely measure up to my expectations. This is especially true of my loved ones, whom I often expect to be perfect even though I am far from perfect myself.

In the Families Anonymous program, as I learned that my Higher Power speaks to me through other people, I tried to listen more carefully to what others had to say.

Now when I start to feel hurt about a remark made to me, I can stop, listen more acutely, and ask myself, "Is this something my Higher Power wants me to hear so that I'll learn something new about myself? Maybe this is a trait I need to work on. Perhaps there is a lesson here for me."

Even someone else's tiresome complaints may contain a challenge for my patience and a chance to practice my program.

TODAY I WILL listen for the lessons life can teach.

Resentments

Resentments are destructive. They impede our recovery from unhealthy, codependent relationships. When we resent others, we lose valuable time, for our resentments become excuses and emotional barriers to knowing ourselves. Resentments can block a healthy relationship, swallow up our efforts to grow, and rob us of the freedom from blame and guilt that is necessary for recovery.

In Families Anonymous, we learn from studying the Twelve Steps how to give up resentments that would otherwise sap us of our will and impede our growth. When we work Step One, we have the key to letting our resentments go.

Forgiveness of others and of ourselves allows us to reclaim responsibility for our own fate. It lets us abandon our opinions and our compulsion to control. By giving up resentments, I can create for myself a new way to live. Letting go of resentments rewards me with inner peace.

TODAY I WILL lay at least one resentment to rest.

September 24

Important Steps

For me, the very foundation of the Families Anonymous program is the first three Steps: I admit I'm powerless, I come to have faith, and I turn my life and will over to a Higher Power.

These Steps helped me with the ones that followed. When I got bogged down in writing my Fourth Step inventory, I stopped and prayed about these first three Steps. This helped me go on. Step Five was easier and more meaningful because I surrendered my pride and accepted my powerlessness with the help of Steps One, Two, and Three.

As I faced Steps Six and Seven, I acknowledged my powerlessness over my character defects. I came to believe that God could remove them, and I humbly put God in charge of doing so, if and when it was in accordance with His will.

Moving along on Steps Eight and Nine, I balked at making amends to one particular person on my list. Again, I applied Steps One, Two, and Three. I knew my Higher Power would provide an opportunity to clear away that remnant of my troublesome past. Quite unexpectedly, I saw a chance to speak to the person, and she graciously accepted my apology and acknowledged her own part in our conflicts.

TODAY I WILL apply the first three Steps to any problem that I encounter.

Stings

We have all heard of that certain species of bee that dies after stinging an enemy. When we sting a loved one with a barbed remark, we are doing ourselves an injury too. And the more often we deliver such repeated "stings," the closer we ourselves come to a moral and spiritual death.

When we are hurt, our first reaction is to get even. But if we step back and look at the situation rationally, trying to get even with someone who's ill makes no sense. *To get even* means to descend to the same level as the one who is ill.

Do we really want to sink to the same level as the addict in our lives, or do we want to help him or her—and help ourselves—attain that higher level where getting even doesn't exist?

The bee stings to destroy its enemy. In Families Anonymous, we give up having enemies and look for friends instead. We do this by working the Twelve Steps and being ever mindful that our loved one is not an enemy. If we have an enemy at all, it is the use of mind-altering drugs—and over such an enemy, we can wield only the weapons of understanding and love.

TODAY I WILL make no remark that might sting another person. Instead, I will try to understand.

September 26

Freedom

As Families Anonymous members, we are quick to recognize that substance abuse has enslaved our loved ones. Yet we do not recognize that our own obsessions keep *us* in bondage. We talk about having a better life, and we truly want it; but as fallible human beings, we ourselves are still sometimes compulsive, angry, self-pitying, and bitter.

It is critical for me to examine the compulsive way I react to certain people or situations. I must admit that, at times, I still nag, scold, cry, and give in to moodiness. If I can recognize these reactions as my own forms of enslavement, I may develop compassion for my loved one's struggles. I too must ask my Higher Power to help me, so that little by little, one step at a time, I can loosen the chains of my shortcomings.

TODAY I WILL recognize my own bonds of slavery—compulsions, anger, and other defects—and ask my Higher Power to set me free.

Who, Me?

I nearly walked out of my first Families Anonymous meeting when a member gently suggested that I needed to be "detoxed" from my chronic enabling. He told me I was addicted to a person with a problem. Addicted? Me? From my perspective, I was exhibiting responsible, adult behavior, trying to straighten out another person.

At the end of the meeting I heard, "...take the thoughts you can accept and leave the rest." My feathers were still ruffled, but after hearing that, I decided to stick around for a while and see how the program worked.

Six months later, exhausted from my vigil over a family member's self-destructive behavior, I finally understood that early suggestion. I was addicted, obsessed with reforming another person, and in the process my own life had become unmanageable.

With the help of FA meetings and many phone calls to other members, I soon replaced my obsession with study of the Twelve Steps, frequent repetition of the Serenity Prayer, and careful attention to my own needs.

TODAY I WILL work for my own recovery from addiction to another person's problems.

September 28

Beginner's Luck

Soon after my first Families Anonymous meeting, I realized I was not "doing it right." I still enabled my addicted child in various ways. I succumbed easily to her manipulations.

Knowing that I wasn't following the program, I sat silently in meetings, feeling uncomfortable and guilty. I wanted to quit going, but for some reason I kept on. Today I'm really glad I did.

With time, I developed a little spunk and began, in small ways, to say *no* to the addict and *yes* to myself.

"No, I will not pay your traffic fine."

"Yes, I will stop fretting over her slovenly habits."

When I shared these experiences in meetings, newer members seemed to gain strength from my accounts. And I continued to grow stronger myself, encouraged by the progress of those who were further into the program than I.

TODAY I WILL remember that I didn't get this way overnight, and that it will take time, patience, and study to recover.

When All Else Fails…

I willingly attended Families Anonymous meetings, seeking help in my struggle with our family's problems. I never missed a meeting. I served as literature chairman and gave great lip service to the program. But life at home seemed as insane as ever. This self-help group had apparently not changed anything.

When I told a close friend in the group that I was ready to stop attending, he asked me whether I had *done* any of the Steps. I knew the Steps, I told him; I could recite all twelve from memory.

"But have you *taken* any of the Steps?" my friend asked. "Have you discussed Step One with yourself? Sometimes it helps to clarify your thinking by writing about it. Have you given your Higher Power a chance to guide you? Have you written an inventory, made a list of persons you've harmed, or made any amends?"

I was forced to admit I had only talked the Steps, not walked them. I began to put on paper how I hated being powerless and how I felt about a life I could not control or manage. I continued to study and write about how I could apply the Steps to my life. I finally achieved more than a speaking acquaintance with the Twelve Steps.

TODAY I WILL study, think, write about, and act upon the Step that is right for my current situation.

September 30

Having a Life

When a very ill patient with cardiac disease is hooked up to an electronic heart-monitoring device, the lines on the screen can tell us that the patient is alive. They dart up and down, carrying the message, "Yes, this heart still beats."

The ups and downs in our daily existence also tell us we are vital, performing individuals. We take risks. We venture out. We give and receive love. Sometimes we despair, but at other times we know great joy.

When a heart monitor shows a perfectly straight line, doctors and nurses know the heart has stopped beating. In the same way, when our lives are smoothed out and nothing ruffles the surface, we have stopped living. We have avoided conflict and risks. There is no pain, no joy. We have isolated ourselves, neither giving nor receiving love.

Which shall we choose—lifeless isolation, or active participation in life?

TODAY I WILL choose to live fully, accepting life on life's terms, in all its energetic vitality.

Live and Let Live

When I truly believe that I am powerless over drugs, alcohol, and other people's lives, I can stop grappling with the problems of my loved one and be free to enjoy my own life at last.

On the other hand, unless I start by concentrating on living, it's hard for me to let go. I need to focus on the first part of this slogan: *Live and let live.*

Intent on living my own life with joy and active participation, I'll have little time left to worry about another person's struggles and scrapes.

If I focus on my own recovery, I'll be too busy to direct another's. When I am fully occupied with *living,* I'll find it easier to *let live.*

TODAY I WILL cultivate my own interests and live in the NOW.

October 2

Now—Today

A wise person said, "He who has one eye on yesterday and one eye on tomorrow sees not clearly today."

One thing I surely cannot change is the past. Regretting the past or searching it to find out where I went wrong does nothing to enhance my present, nor does it offer a chance to correct my mistakes. My intentions have been good for the most part.

I can plan my own future activities, but no amount of worrying will influence future outcomes. My worrying will not solve another person's problems, and it only creates problems for me.

That leaves today, this moment, for me to live, love, work, and enjoy. All I have is this moment.

TODAY I WILL live in the NOW.

Acceptance

Acceptance does not mean that I have to be a doormat. I do not have to accept the unacceptable. I can expect others to respect my rights, as I respect theirs.

I can try to keep a clear picture of my responsibilities and let others take care of their own. When I hurt, I can say *ouch*. I can remove myself from intolerable situations.

For me, acceptance means that I will live life on life's terms. Certain realities, such as disease, natural disasters, and how others choose to live, are beyond my control. I cannot change them. Acceptance of reality will bring me closer to my goal of serenity.

TODAY I WILL keep my goal of serenity in mind as I weigh what I must accept and what I don't have to accept.

October 4

Changing What I Can

Before coming to Families Anonymous, I used to talk my head off about "The Problem." Although I heard people's sighs and saw the pity mixed with annoyance on their faces, I rattled on anyway. I lied to my family and covered up many incidents. I was angry much of the time and nervous about getting caught in my lies. Unable to handle such chaos, I became even angrier.

Then I found FA and walked through the door of hope. I began to be aware of my anger, self-pity, compulsive talking, and lies. I realized that I was impatient, gave unwanted advice, and didn't listen. I didn't like to face my defects of character.

The program is helping me change many of these shortcomings. My negative attitudes have been replaced by a more positive way of thinking and feeling about myself. I now take better care of *me*. I am more understanding, see the good in others, and accept the things I cannot change.

TODAY I WILL have the courage to change the things I can.

Step One

We admitted we were powerless over drugs and other people's lives, that our lives had become unmanageable.

For most of us, this was the hardest Step to take. As parents, we firmly believed that we could and should control and direct our children. That was our responsibility. But when we reviewed the insane life we were living, it became plain we were not in control of our children or of ourselves. Our lives *were* unmanageable.

The more we tried to take control, the crazier things got. All the dire threats and warnings, all the snooping and checking didn't work at all. We had to admit we *were* powerless.

What a relief that admission was! We *weren't* dismal failures, rotten parents, or vindictive maniacs. We were sincere, helpless people who had come up against something beyond our control.

Once we accept and absorb this Step, we can begin to work on the one thing within our power—ourselves. Our peace of mind hinges on admitting our own powerlessness over others and claiming the ability to change ourselves.

TODAY I WILL accept my powerlessness over the life of any other person.

October 6

Self-Pity

After some pretty rough treatment from a member of my family, I wanted to return to my old ways of reacting. She was really pushing my buttons! I knew I had to do something to keep from losing my serenity.

I went outside with a book of daily meditations and opened it to a page on self-pity. Before I began reading, I had thought I was justified in pitying myself because of the way I was being treated. I felt sorry for myself because my husband was dealing with the situation better than I was, and he didn't understand why I was having such a hard time. I resented him for not understanding, and I resented the fact that I bore so many of the insults.

What I read helped me see that I was defeating myself through self-pity. I could stay there and continue to be miserable, or I could move on. I had legitimate reasons for feeling hurt, but I could break the cycle if I wanted to. Even though the situation didn't change, I felt as though a big weight had been lifted from me when I realized I could choose how to respond.

TODAY I WILL choose to let hurt and self-pity go.

Whom Have We Harmed?

At a Families Anonymous meeting, we were studying Step Eight: *Made a list of all persons we had harmed and became willing to make amends to them all.* One member resisted. *"He's* the one who should make amends to *me*," she said. "I don't have to apologize for anything."

A gentle old-timer spoke up. "I like to think my daughter is making amends to me by taking charge of her own life and staying clean and sober—though, of course, she has to do it only for herself. As for me, I need to make amends to my wife for all the times I blamed her for failures in our household. I have to forgive myself for lying to cover up our problems. My co-workers go on the list because I was ill-tempered and intolerant in my relationship with them. Why, I think I'll even put you on my list, because I may be judging you at this moment, even though I once felt just as you do."

Our resistant member smiled, relaxed, and continued to listen.

TODAY I WILL search my memory for all the persons I may have harmed, then plan to make amends to them.

October 8

Happiness

When his grandfather asked what he wished for, a young boy answered, "Happiness! What would you wish for, Grandpa?"

"Well," said the elder, "I have everything I need right now, but if I could go back to the time when I was your age, I'd wish to *know* when I'm happy. Today, when I look back, I remember times when I didn't know how good life was. I was too busy griping and worrying about whether I'd ever get a bicycle or a yo-yo or a saxophone. I didn't take time to enjoy my family, my home, a good joke, the garden, my friends, or even the smell of morning."

This man had learned that we are most likely to discover happiness when we stop looking for it as an end in itself. It is a by-product of grateful, wide-awake living.

TODAY I WILL try to not dwell on anything that keeps me from enjoying my blessings.

Higher Power

After a crisis, when life has returned to normal (if there is such a thing), I can easily fall back into my old habits. I can relapse into living without keeping conscious contact with my Higher Power.

We all know those fair-weather friends who stick around only so long as life is rosy. I can easily become a "bad-weather friend" of my Higher Power, making contact only when I need help.

In my study and practice of the Families Anonymous program, I am reminded to stay close to the source of my serenity. It's essential that I remember to express gratitude at all times—but especially when I'm relatively free of problems. And seeking daily spiritual guidance makes me ready to be an instrument of God's will.

Experience teaches me that when I live the FA program and stay in touch with a Higher Power on a daily basis, my crises will be fewer and farther apart.

TODAY I WILL stay aware of my Higher Power.

October 10

Changes

At one of our Families Anonymous meetings, a member who had been with us for six months said, "The FA program has convinced me to let go of some old ideas. My son doesn't *have* to go to college right away. Maybe he'll never go. How do I know what he needs? I must let him decide."

She went on. "I'm teaching myself to change by doing many things differently—putting my right shoe on first instead of the left one, taking a walk before breakfast instead of rushing into the kitchen, and getting up earlier to manage it. I've changed my hair style and bought new clothes. I even rearranged the furniture. It may seem silly, but doing these things helps me feel like a new me in a new place!"

TODAY I WILL look closely at my old ways, keep the valuable ones, and let go of those that are useless.

Honesty

Sharing experiences in Families Anonymous meetings is as beneficial to the giver as it is to the receiver. It is the beginning of an attempt to be honest, perhaps for the first time in years.

I often feel cleansed of guilt when I admit some fault or mistake in judgment. I am released from a self-made prison in which I had no one with whom to share my deepest feelings.

I may not always identify with the experience being shared in a meeting, but it frequently strikes a common chord. If I listen attentively, with humility, I can often receive flashes of insight into my own life. Staying with the topic of discussion, I can help others by sharing my experiences too. In so doing, I also help myself.

TODAY I WILL be open and honest about myself and my reactions.

October 12

Smooth Sailing?

Families Anonymous helps us chart the way out of the stormy sea of life. After years of turmoil, it takes us a while to reach calm waters, the safe harbor of serenity.

But at times, all that calmness makes me uncomfortable. I've grown used to excitement, and now there is no helm for me to grab. No one needs me to be captain. It doesn't feel right. I crave the challenge of taking charge. Sometimes I even stir things up a bit without realizing it.

Then I remember I have a job to do—working my program. I get busy and read my FA literature again, get back on course, release the people around me, stop controlling, and sail back into FA's "serenity harbor."

When I took an honest look at my need for challenge, control, and leadership, I realized I was addicted to being in charge. Without enumerating the life experiences that made me this way, let me just say that I'm learning, through the Twelve Step program, to turn over the helm to a better captain—my Higher Power. By doing so, I learn to appreciate calm waters as opposed to bucking stormy seas. Practicing the Steps and applying them to all my affairs is the surest course to serenity.

TODAY I WILL practice not taking charge but instead will entrust the voyage to my Higher Power.

Circles of Communication

In Families Anonymous, we learn to avoid adding to another person's guilt and lack of self-worth. Our relationships at home improve when we learn to deal productively with our anger and to rethink our verbal responses to the misbehaviors of our loved ones.

Some of us make the mistake of discussing our loved ones with relatives and friends, wallowing in self-pity and making a bid for sympathy for ourselves.

One of the consequences of this practice is that the "news" makes the rounds and often gets back to the people we were discussing, detracting even more from their self-esteem.

If we must expose our problems to outsiders, we can do so by stressing our concern for our loved ones. Anyone afflicted with the disease of alcoholism or addiction is already suffering enough without having to suffer my criticism and complaints as well.

TODAY I WILL confide in a trusted FA friend if I need to talk about a problem.

October 14

Appreciation

When we do something good for someone else, we want to experience that goodness being given back to us. But we often experience just the opposite. We may give time and energy to others and receive little or no appreciation. We are taken for granted, or else people use us and go their own way without so much as a "Thank you." Is it possible that this lack of appreciation stems from the fact that we're offering "help" where no help is wanted?

Still, there *are* other people in our lives who do respond in warm ways, often giving much more to us than we've given to them. These people we may forget quickly. Why then is it so hard to forgive those who slight us? Is it because we have an exaggerated sense of how deserving we are?

I find the best approach is to concentrate on all the love, assistance, friendliness, and welcome I receive, allowing everything else to fade into the distance.

TODAY I WILL be grateful for every kindness and take no blessing for granted.

Advice

The Families Anonymous program reminds us to stop, listen, and think. It warns us specifically against giving advice. In our struggles of daily living, we have all seen that most advice is not welcomed, accepted, or followed. It is, in fact, often resented, challenged, disputed, and ignored.

Rather than giving advice at meetings, FA members share their own life experiences. Sharing places us on common ground, allowing others the freedom to accept or reject what we've said.

But our *program* does not lack guideposts. The Twelve Steps, Twelve Traditions, and readings that begin each FA meeting are the sound principles of our program. They invite us to give up our ego-driven anger, blame, and efforts to control or manipulate. The program encourages us to seek to know the Higher Power of our personal choice and rely upon that Power as a constant guide. The Twelve Steps help us learn to know ourselves and get on with our own lives.

TODAY I WILL neither ask for nor give advice but instead will follow the wisdom of the program.

October 16

Whose Approval Do I Need?

I wanted my children's friends to like me, so I used to play the part of "cool mom" to perfection. I was good for a laugh. That was okay. Young folks liked to pour out their troubles for my sympathy. Nothing wrong there.

But I looked the other way when kids did things at my house that I knew they couldn't do at home. Sometimes they drank at our house. One boy even grew a funny-looking plant in our back yard.

When I found my way to Families Anonymous, it became important for me to get honest. When I took a look at what I was doing with regard to my children's friends, I saw that I was behaving just the way teenagers in a gang behave when trying to be popular. I was neglecting my own adult standards and values as I grasped for young Joe's or Julie's approval!

I was in error when I allowed young people to do things in my home that were destructive, let alone illegal. I was not being fair to them or their parents. I was not being true to myself. Working my FA program today, I need only my own approval and the knowledge that I am dealing honestly with the issues of life.

TODAY I WILL be a responsible parent instead of a runner-up in a meaningless popularity contest.

Silence

From attending Families Anonymous meetings, I've decided that there are times when I must be quiet, say nothing, and do nothing.

I find it hard to keep still when my mind is in turmoil. My lips want to scream out volumes of reproach and resentments. At such times, I am learning to take deep breaths to help me relax my body and open my mind to rational thoughts. Then, to squelch these negative thoughts, I do some thinking along program lines. I might silently ask, "What Step or slogan do I need to concentrate on right now?"

Sometimes I just say the Serenity Prayer over and over silently. Still other ways I work with silence are to recall some pleasant experience I've had or to imagine an event I'm looking forward to.

TODAY I WILL try making my silences beneficial to me rather than a punishment to others.

October 18

The Serenity of Boundaries

When I first encountered the Families Anonymous e-meeting, the hardest lesson for me was learning to say *no*. My son/addict had an almost daily catastrophe that often required additional funding. It took time and work with my sponsor for me to grasp that giving into my son's demands prolonged his illness, making life easy for him. Though I thought that I was *helping* him, I was actually giving him more money to spend on drugs. He was dying before my eyes, and I too was slipping away.

Gradually I learned that my boundaries were meant to protect *my serenity*. They were not meant to cure or control my son. I kept my boundaries simple, with enforceable consequences. I said, "You must find a job within ten days." "No using in our home." "Be home by midnight." With the support of my sponsor, I stuck to my boundaries, even during very heart-wrenching pleas for assistance.

In time, my son proved that he could not abide by my boundaries and was asked to move out. He left town to live with friends, and gradually his life began to improve.

During a recent visit, my son thanked me for being firm with him. Thanks to my FA program and sponsor, I was able to find the serenity that had previously eluded me. As an added bonus, I was able to give my son the dignity to live life on his terms.

TODAY I WILL use my knowledge of boundaries to help me in all aspects of my life.

The Art of Being Serene

Being serene is an art, and like any other art, it can be mastered. Serenity is not a creative art, but a learning art, like the art of cooking or carpentry. Like these other arts, the art of serenity has two parts: theory and practice.

We in Families Anonymous are fortunate to have the theory of serenity spelled out for us. Our Twelve Steps are the formula that will lead us to serenity. Slogans and other program readings reinforce the Steps and provide a solid foundation for the theory of serenity. That's the easy part. Putting this theory into practice is a bit more difficult.

Reading a cookbook does not make one a cook. And learning the slogans, the Serenity Prayer, and the Steps does not lead to instant serenity. Only by putting what we have learned into practice will we attain even the smallest measure of serenity. Some of us will learn more quickly than others, but if we follow the "recipes" and the "blueprints" FA provides, we will surely find serenity.

TODAY I WILL study the theory and practice the art of serenity.

October 20

Walking Away

Walking away may seem like a bad idea, but there are times when it's both desirable and necessary. When others criticize unfairly, blame, or abuse me verbally, I can always choose simply to walk away.

We've all heard that "sticks and stones may break my bones, but words will never hurt me." When a verbal attack takes place, however, accusations, threats, and put-downs are hard to ignore. They hurt! They're especially painful when inflicted by friends and loved ones or by people we have worked diligently to help.

When we're suddenly and unexpectedly confronted with such stressful situations, our best defense may be to remind ourselves that just because someone says it's so doesn't make it so. We may have to prepare this simple defense well in advance of any crisis; but, forewarned and forearmed, we have a better-than-even chance of walking away, at least mentally, when we're suddenly confronted with an unfair or unkind attack.

TODAY I WILL remember that walking away from conflict may be one way to detach.

Learning About Me

Who am I, and what do I want? Before I came into the Families Anonymous program, I was so wrapped up in the lives of others that I had no reply to these questions. But now I'm learning more about myself. I know that there is peace in solitude, as opposed to pain in loneliness, and I am learning to enjoy being alone, a wonderful new experience.

Early in the morning, I walk with my dog. I am alone with my thoughts at these special times. I notice the shapes of the trees and the shadows they cast. I hear the early-morning bird calls. I pass silent, sleeping houses and wonder about the people within.

I see a carefully tended garden and consider the people who planted and care for it. I promise myself to thank them for the beauty they have brought to this place. I'm more in tune with the universe because, in this program, I have addressed my shortcomings and know myself better.

I am happy to be me, grateful to be learning more about myself.

TODAY I WILL be at peace with my new friend: myself.

October 22

Serenity

It takes us a while in Families Anonymous to learn that the goal of this program is serenity for ourselves. It would be wonderful to see our loved ones happy and whole, but we lack the power to bring this about. And if we try to control others and tell them how to live, we are doomed to frustration and despair. We are diverted from our quest for serenity.

The best thing we can do is turn our friends and relatives over to the care of a Power greater than ourselves. We can make a careful study of the Serenity Prayer and perhaps even make a list of the things we can change—as well as a list of the "unchangeables." Then we can express our gratitude by getting on with the day-to-day business of living, ever mindful that the most important thing in our lives is our serenity.

TODAY I WILL seek serenity by committing myself to a full and satisfying life.

Living in the Now

When my children were small, I spent most of my time waiting for something to be over: teething, the "terrible twos," adolescence. I was forever living in a fantasy of the future. Then came long weeks and months when I waited for my middle child to give up her destructive use of alcohol.

At last I came to Families Anonymous. Here I learned to live and enjoy my life *today*, forgetting about that uncertain future. Having learned to let my children go, I'm cultivating the best today that I can, no longer hooking my happiness onto someone else's performance. No more postponing the realization of my *own* potentials! I'm tapping them now with guitar lessons. I no longer live in the strain of hoping that "Tomorrow will be better day," for if I did, I would be sacrificing a perfectly good today.

TODAY I WILL remember that **now** is the real thing and not a dress rehearsal.

October 24

What If…?

"What if…?" This seems to be another one of the unavoidable stops on the road to recovery.

"What if my son starts using again?" "What if he chooses the wrong friends?" "What if he stops going to AA?" I can work myself into a frenzy with those two little words—if I choose to do so.

"What if" is a hard place to get past, but in Families Anonymous we know we have to push on and leave it behind. If I determine simply to live this moment, this hour, this day, joyfully and serenely, I need never bother with "what if" again. When I fall back on "what if," I am projecting a future that may never happen.

I will let two other words—"thank God"—take the place of "what if," finding at least one thing to be grateful for today and focusing on it—my own good health, a bird's song, a child's laughter, and especially Families Anonymous.

TODAY I WILL let my negatives be replaced by positives, my fear by faith, and "what if" by "thank God."

Detachment

The topic for the FA meeting was *detachment*. Each member was asked to write a short statement about it. Here are some of them:

Detachment is…

- taking a hands-off attitude and letting the person fend for himself
- minding my own business when she procrastinates on important business matters
- letting go of another person to be and do as that person chooses in all areas of his life
- choosing not to rescue, but rather to believe that he can succeed
- finding a good habit to replace my bad habit of worrying
- declining to tell my friend what to do, while supporting her confidence in her own decisions
- letting go of my guilt when my daughter makes disastrous choices
- ceasing to be the provider for my adult children
- accepting that I cannot live my children's lives for them but *can* continue to love them dearly and want the best for them
- helping my child stand on her own two feet, without buying the shoes forever

TODAY I WILL practice detaching with love.

October 26

Rituals

Use whatever works! A member of Families Anonymous tells what helps her to let go: "I have a small ritual I perform to help me get off the merry-go-round of worry. Imagining that the on/off switch for worry is an arm's length away, I simply reach out my hand and turn it off. Then I actually take a step forward, as if to get off the whirling carousel of endless fretting."

When another member has a problem, he writes a letter to his Higher Power. He then puts the paper in a special container he calls a "God Box." He laughs and says, "It sounds spooky, but it works! Sometimes I realize, weeks later, that the problem has worked itself out."

"I go for a walk," says a woman whose husband is an addict, "repeating over and over, *Let go and let God.* I always return feeling better."

TODAY I WILL do whatever it takes to feel sane and serene.

Foundations

I felt as if the "house" of my life was crumbling. Those solid walls, which I had thought were so sturdy, had been built around illusion. The foundation was based on dreams and worthless schemes. The whole structure weakened during days of indecision and nights of anguish and fear. The edifice that had been my life seemed to totter and collapse before my very eyes. All attempts to shore it up failed. I felt naked and exposed.

When all my attempts to put my house in order proved futile, I gave up the struggle and turned in despair to my Higher Power. By then I had lost the urge to plead and ask why. I had abandoned the wasteful anger and useless threats against those who had destroyed my sanctuary. Brought to rock bottom, I was ready to start all over again.

The architect of my rebuilding was my Higher Power; my foundation, a lasting one, was the Twelve Steps. Using the strength of changed attitudes and the support of firm resolve, I've built a comfortable dwelling place in which to live out the rest of my days.

TODAY I WILL share with someone else the new life that can be built on the foundation of the Twelve Step program of Families Anonymous.

October 28

Responsibility

Assuming a protective role, I once kept my chemically dependent loved one sequestered from life, wrapped up in a cocoon of my own needs. I used to nurture this person in a cradle I called "responsibility," which in reality was my own guilt and my need to manage and control.

In Families Anonymous, I've come to see myself in a new light. My Twelve Step program is helping me modify these restrictive old habits and traits. I try to remember that whether my loved one is sober or not, his personality is still his own. He can still be trapped by mood swings—both his and mine—as well as by my overeagerness to become involved in his life, using an inappropriate system of punishments and rewards.

The best thing for me to remember is to *love and let be*. Progress will surely result if I give *credit for attempts at progress and for having had many victories which are unknown.*

TODAY I WILL remember: I can change myself. Others I can only love.

Taking Care of Me

One of my character defects has been overdoing the caretaker role. I used to try to take care of everybody *but* me, and in the process I was destroying myself.

Since I found Families Anonymous, I've learned that taking care of *me* is the only thing that makes sense if I am to grow and find serenity. It's not selfish; it's sensible. If I love myself, I can love others too.

I'm taking care of myself when I refuse to stay up all night worrying about someone else. I'm taking care of myself when I eat healthy meals, regardless of whether anyone else is home or not. I do it for me, because I deserve it.

Nobody can take as good care of me as I can. Some of the ways I care for me are by…

- attending FA meetings regularly
- setting aside a few minutes each day to meditate and pray
- taking the time to go out with friends
- inviting a friend to lunch
- claiming a day to do as I please, without guilt
- devoting time to my hobby
- taking a long, leisurely bubble bath
- going for a walk, reading, or just sitting in the sun
- focusing on positive ideas and attitudes
- treating myself to a trip

TODAY I WILL take good care of myself, knowing that loving myself is good practice for loving others.

October 30

Easy Does It

My standard response to life has always been to get worked up over everything. Laid back, I'm not! I have strong opinions, know just how things ought to be done, am bothered by unpredictable events, and find it painful to adapt to change. With me, everything has always been a federal case.

Always, that is, until I came to Families Anonymous. Here I made a wonderful discovery—a slogan that goes, *Easy does it.* Why do those three words seem so wonderful? It's because they have completely changed my life.

Easy does it means many things. It means I don't have to know all the answers. I can listen instead of speak. I can let someone else have the last word. I can let another person head the committee. The problem need not be solved today. I can take ten minutes out from my work, sit down with a cold lemonade, and enjoy watching the birds at the feeder.

Easy does it means taking several slow, deep breaths before saying the first angry word. It means thinking things over instead of acting in haste. It means sitting down at the table, eating slowly, and appreciating the food. It means trusting in my Higher Power, all day and all night.

TODAY I WILL see how many ways *Easy does it* can work for me.

Ghosts

Halloween, a festival with roots in antiquity, is a time when the spirits of all the departed were said to roam the earth.

For many of us, "ghosts" of the past are still very much alive. Any member of Families Anonymous can tell you that not every "ghost" of bygone days or bygone events has been laid to rest.

What are some of the "ghosts" of your past? Are they your regrets for things you wish you hadn't done—or things you wish you had done? Are they highly charged emotions you haven't processed— emotions like anger, resentment, or fear? One of my "ghosts" used to be the fear that my child would return to drinking and using drugs. I lived with that "ghost" on a daily basis, until I decided to turn the clear light of reality upon it and let it evaporate into nothingness.

Perhaps one of your "ghosts" is the memory of a parent who treated you in a harsh or abusive way. Perhaps there's the "shade" of someone who got something you wanted while you were ignored. Maybe you're haunted by the "spook" of someone who was your youngster's partner in the misuse of drugs.

Whatever these "ghosts" are, they have power over our lives only so long as we give them that power. Living today is the only way to have a life.

TODAY I WILL bury the past and put all my "ghosts" to rest.

November 1

…Let Me Count the Ways

The Families Anonymous program has helped me in more ways than I can count. Some of these are the gifts of growth, self-esteem, love, and peace. My daily life is better as long as I keep coming back to meetings, studying the literature, and working the Steps.

A special joy is seeing the newcomers who need the program so desperately. Their presence also reminds me how far I've come from the depth of despair that was once the common experience of us all.

By sharing my recovery with a newcomer, either by phone or at meetings, I live serenely, day by day, in spite of the many inevitable ups and downs.

TODAY I WILL be grateful for the countless ways in which FA has improved my life.

Change

An addict cannot be forced to change. Change happens only when he or she reaches that point we call *hitting bottom.* The person then recognizes, deep down inside, that the pain of the addicted life is too great to be endured a moment longer. That is when the addict's recovery begins.

When we relatives and friends come to the inner realization that the pain of our own lives can no longer be endured and that our unproductive and sometimes insane reactions have to change, we too start to get well. Our healthier attitudes and reactions demonstrate to the addicts in our lives that they can't "con" us anymore. If they are determined to con anyone, it can only be themselves.

We cannot bring about change in anyone else. We can only love others, detaching from their problems but not from them as human beings. We can love ourselves enough to carry on and live our own lives, in spite of the fact that others may never choose what we want for them.

TODAY I WILL be grateful for my growing inner peace, knowing that recovery comes from within.

November 3

From a Sister

Having a sister who's an addict is very hard, but Families Anonymous has helped me learn many new ways of coping with my feelings about her.

Before FA, I would do anything to be my sister's friend. I thought I was helping her by keeping secrets and lying. At the time, I couldn't see what I was doing, but now I know I was really hurting her.

During my short time in FA, I have learned to not be the go-between for my parents and sister. Now I step back and let them encounter each other. They don't always do what I think they should, but I know I cannot prescribe their actions, buffer their feelings, or tell them what to say. When I find it too painful to witness their mistakes, I remove myself from the scene, let go, and pray they get through these horrendous experiences, one way or another.

It was in an FA meeting that I found the strength to do this. Another member said, "I finally learned that I cannot take away another person's pain."

TODAY I WILL take care of my own feelings and allow others to bear responsibility for theirs.

November 4

From a Brother

Before I came to Families Anonymous, I had let my life become a catastrophe because of my brother's drug abuse. I always thought I was supposed to help him do whatever he wanted, because he was my brother.

When my brother went into a treatment center, I participated in the family phase of his program and learned to cope with problems more successfully. Now, instead of living by my brother's demands, I let my own conscience help me decide what to do. Today I try to live my life as an individual rather than as one half of a twosome (my brother and me).

After his treatment, my brother began to attend his own support group meetings. I found my way to FA, and I'm surely glad I did. FA has helped me continue to grow into a caring but *independent* person. I am working on my own recovery. No matter whether my brother succeeds in his recovery, no matter whether he goes to meetings, I continue to attend as many FA meetings as I can.

TODAY I WILL make the most of my own life, one day at a time.

November 5

Choices

We all have choices. My loved ones need to be given the dignity to make their own choices. I can give them that dignity by telling them, "You are free to make your own choices," and mean it.

But since I have a right to choose light instead of darkness and serenity instead of insanity, I must also give them the dignity of *learning from* their choices. "I'll always love you," I tell them, "but the consequences of your choices will be yours to contend with. I owe you that freedom."

However, I will not speak these thoughts until I am *strong* enough to carry through on them.

TODAY I WILL make choices for myself and leave others the dignity of making their own.

Silence

One day I was having a particularly hard time trying to not react to someone's attacks on me. I recalled something I had heard at a Families Anonymous meeting: "I don't have to have the last word."

Remembering this really helped me defuse the situation as the attacker was yelling insults at me. I chose to not react in the ways I had reacted before. This time, I silently prayed to get through the incident with dignity. Things calmed down because I had not added fuel to the fire.

Sometimes silence really is golden. So that my silence won't appear to another as sulking or rejection, I busy my mind in thinking about some helpful part of the FA program: a Step, a slogan, or the Serenity Prayer.

TODAY I WILL speak only when my words are an improvement on silence.

November 7

I Can Change Myself

I used to be so entangled in my children's lives that I never gave a thought to my own life. If they were doing well, I felt successful. And when my children had problems, I became fixated on finding solutions for them.

My son really tested everyone. When I had to ask him to leave my house, he moved in with his dad. Wearing out his welcome there, he went to live with a clergyman who was sure he could turn him around. Then the boy disappeared, leaving a suicide note behind.

Police and relatives searched out my son and forced him into a hospital. For a time after that, I assumed my old role of trying to run his life. Fortunately, in the hospital I heard about Families Anonymous.

As I began to study and practice the Twelve Steps of FA, I learned that I could turn things over to God, allow my son to manage his life, and direct my energies to managing my own.

Today my son is still floundering, but I'm not. Instead of projecting into a frightening future, I live one day at a time with a serenity I never knew before. In place of my old guilt, I know courage. I no longer feel isolated, because I am certain of my rightful place in the world. I have a reason to belong.

TODAY I WILL let my loved ones choose their own destinies, and I will create a future of my own.

Working the Program

People in my Families Anonymous meeting talk about *working the program.* "What does this mean?" I asked. A member answered kindly, "For me, *working the program* means living the Twelve Steps—not just saying the words at meetings, but admitting, believing, and doing the Steps to the best of my ability." That was his answer.

After several years in FA, my own answer has become, "*Working the program* means continual self-discovery and self-improvement."

Changing myself is never easy, whether it's changing my attitudes, my negativity, my reactions, my lazy habits, or some other aspect of myself.

I've tried to say good-bye to fear, anger, guilt, worry, hate, violence, profanity, sarcasm, suspicion, directing, and expecting. These were not easy to give up; but thanks to this program, I have been able to say hello to faith, forgiveness, acceptance, love, patience, my Higher Power, and the goodness in other people.

TODAY I WILL continue to define what *working the program* means in my life.

November 9

Try Listening—It Helps!

When I first started attending Families Anonymous meetings, I was looking for an easy solution to my two sons' problems. But after months of hitting my head against the same old stone wall—my attitude—I started to listen more carefully at meetings. I soon heard that FA is not for my sons but for me. Any solutions I find must therefore apply to *me*.

My sons' problems still exist, but mine have been lessened greatly.

Now I concentrate on responsibility for my own actions and reactions. No longer can I use the problems of others as an excuse to ignore my own. I feel better about myself, have more success in my own endeavors, and find that my failures are fewer and smaller. I am no longer afraid to tackle the personal problems I've been avoiding for years.

I accept the fact today that I cannot change my sons' lives, and I have stopped hindering them in their growth.

TODAY I WILL not be afraid to face myself and my own problems.

Codependency

Codependency can be defined as an obsession with controlling the behavior of others. Along with that fact goes another: a codependent person may also *be controlled* by the behavior of others.

Many of us tend to become codependent in our relationships with our loved ones. We end up rescuing, enabling, or caretaking as a way of life. I call it the "Coast Guard complex." The Coast Guard rescues people; that's part of their job. But does it necessarily have to be mine?

When rescuing people in peril, a person may find that his or her own life is expendable. Do I suffer from the Coast Guard complex, believing it's okay to sacrifice myself in order to rescue others from disasters of their own making?

My role as helper is clearly spelled out in the Families Anonymous reading entitled HELPING, but sometimes I forget and go at it in the wrong way, trying to rescue. And then the Coast Guard complex takes over, with its cargo of resentment, low self-esteem, and a feeling of being victimized. I project blame onto the very person I've tried to rescue. But when I'm practicing my program, I remember in time to read FA literature, call an FA friend, or pray. I restrain myself from rescuing.

TODAY I WILL help instead of rescue—by not doing for other people what they can do for themselves.

November 11

Higher Power

Before I came to Families Anonymous, I had almost given up hope that a Power "greater than ourselves" could make a difference. I had scolded, worried, wept, prayed, and sought counseling, while my son's chemical abuse grew steadily worse.

But that Higher Power made the difference. Away at college, my son reached a time of crisis in his use of drugs. I dropped everything and went to him, lovingly, and for the first time, nonjudgmentally, offered family support for him to go to a treatment center.

Our Higher Power was there ahead of me. My son was ready for help. While under the influence of drugs, he'd heard a voice telling him unmistakably that he must stop using drugs or die. Furthermore, the same voice told him he would be unable to stop without the help of others. His Higher Power had done what I could not do—make my son ready for healing.

From this experience, I realized that a greater plan than my own small one is indeed at work, often operating outside of my awareness. That same Higher Power continues to guide me in my own program of recovery.

TODAY I WILL be grateful for the reality that a Higher Power can and will make the difference.

Keep Coming Back—It Works

Members of a Families Anonymous group tell us why they *keep coming back:*

"If I don't come, something is missing. After four years in the fellowship, I still cannot do the job by myself. I come back just for me."

"The group gives me the tools I need."

"FA helps me in all aspects of my life. I come here to get recharged."

"It makes life more peaceful. I need the warmth, understanding, and support."

"FA reminds me that I don't have to take on every problem around me."

"Meetings keep me centered emotionally and spiritually. My fears and controlling stay manageable, I can stay serene, and I'm reminded to keep contact with my Higher Power."

"Coming here allows me to help others as I have been helped."

"I come to share with caring people and be reminded that my anger can be expressed constructively. I no longer waste energy hating everything that goes wrong."

"Someone always says something that helps. A better way of life is what keeps me coming back."

TODAY I WILL keep coming back. It works!

November 13

How Are You Good to Yourself?

The members of a Families Anonymous group shared the various ways they are good to themselves.

One woman volunteered, "I try not to be like Mighty Mouse–you know, *Here I am to save the day.* I resist coming to the rescue and let others help themselves."

Another parent said, "I concentrate on Step Two— *Came to believe that a power greater than myself could restore me to sanity.* This helps me remember I am powerless, truly powerless, over any other person, place, or thing. It gets the focus back on me and where I need to change."

Still another member chimed in, "I laugh. A sense of humor saves me, when I allow it to, from the effects of some sad experiences. My sense of humor is just as important to me as being serious. How am I good to myself? I answer with a question: *Have I laughed today?*"

Finally someone said simply, "I pray."

TODAY I WILL be good to myself in whatever way works best—but I will be good to myself because I deserve it.

Resentment and Self-Pity

I've come to believe that recovery from codependency must be every bit as hard as recovery from alcoholism or addiction. Giving up the resentment and pain I feel about my wife's addiction is a continual struggle.

Resentment and self-pity are ever-present—yet whenever these feelings surface, they are invariably destructive and depressing. I keep reminding myself to stop looking back, for I can do nothing about the past! I cannot even look to the future. The only moment I *can* do something about is now.

Today I can be grateful that I have learned and grown stronger from my experiences. I can be grateful that I'm not alone, that I am in the company of others who have been through what I have been through, and worse, and have survived. If they have made it, I can make it too.

TODAY I WILL guard against resentment and self-pity, remembering that living today to the fullest is the only way to have a life.

November 15

Anger

I was brought up in a home where everyone either blew up or smoldered. I was terrified of anger—afraid to be near it, express it, or even accept its presence in my own heart. Anger meant rejection, bad feelings, shame, and guilt.

Through Families Anonymous, I have learned to accept the reality of my own anger as well as the fact that another person's anger cannot diminish me.

Anger need not be a violent urge to lash out. Properly expressed, anger can be a force for good. If I am angry enough to say *no*, once and for all, to my addicted child's manipulation, my anger has changed things for the better.

Today I know how to say, "I feel really angry right now. I'll talk with you about it after I've had a chance to think things through."

Anger itself is neither good nor bad. Like all our other feelings, anger just *is*. Ignored, it causes ulcers, high blood pressure, headaches, and depression. Accepted calmly and honestly, properly channeled and expressed, anger can bring about healthful change.

TODAY I WILL give up my fear of anger and let it work for good.

Forgiveness

"Forgive," I was told by members of my Families Anonymous group, and how that rankled! I had no intention of forgiving. I had made a virtual career of nurturing my resentments. I clung to my memories of all the dirty deeds my abuser had perpetrated. And a few other people's slights were carefully noted in my memory bank as well.

I rubbed my old wounds raw, until they festered enough to make me physically ill, spiritually empty, and emotionally dead.

This suffering must have been necessary in order for me to reach the "bottom" they speak of that makes people decide to get well. From the depths of defeat, I found the humility to cry for the help that FA offered. I saw that I could recover only if I let go of resentments through the process of forgiving.

At last! I felt relieved and began to wake up to life.

TODAY I WILL remember that forgiveness is the first phase of healing.

November 17

Be Good to Yourself

Somewhere along the line, I got the crazy idea that everyone but me deserved treats. I thought this went along with being a mom. Aren't we the ones who use the spoon that fell in the garbage disposal, the egg with the broken yolk, the burnt piece of toast, the uncomfortable chair?

I used to do all those things. *But not any more!* When a member of our Families Anonymous group gave a program on being good to yourself, I thought it was such a great idea that I haven't stopped trying it out yet.

How am I good to myself? For starters, instead of going around looking as though I'm wearing a Halloween fright wig, I visit the beauty shop and have my hair cut and styled. I use makeup becomingly. I dress well.

When I'm tired, I ask a family member to massage my back. I go for long, energizing walks, even when the sink is full of dirty dishes. I make time for activities that lift my spirits: listening to peaceful music, writing letters, gardening, reading just for fun, taking a bubble bath. I ask for help when necessary. I surround myself with positive people. Being good to myself is great— and who deserves it more?

TODAY I WILL be good to myself and not feel one bit guilty.

Maintenance

When I buy a maintenance insurance policy on a new appliance, I'm getting peace of mind regarding a large investment. When I work on Steps Ten and Eleven in my Families Anonymous program, I ensure my peace of mind about my investment in life.

I take my inventory daily to prevent the buildup of resentment, anger, guilt, and self-pity. This is vital to my serenity. If I immediately recognize when I am wrong, I can admit it and make amends as necessary.

During a daily inventory, I look for positive actions and reactions and appreciate the progress I've made in my program. I accept myself and others as we are.

The second part of my maintenance is daily prayer and meditation, which keep me in touch with my Higher Power. Prayer and meditation permit me to let go. This is a special time to enjoy my serenity. Without distractions, I can feel and appreciate the calmness and peace resulting from my Twelve Step program.

TODAY I WILL keep my "maintenance insurance policy," the Tenth and Eleventh Steps, up-to-date and in full force.

November 19

Enabling

Providing the means for an addict to practice his or her addiction is called *enabling,* something we in Families Anonymous try to avoid. It's difficult to refuse an abuser's request for food money. Sometimes a relative will actually buy food or pay a landlord rather than give money to the abuser. Many FA members say that even those precautions are self-defeating, because whatever funds the user has are then available for purchasing drugs or alcohol.

Next to putting a sick person out of the house, the toughest stand we may be called upon to take is refusing money for food, rent, or bail. This is a highly personal decision, but many in FA have found that taking such a hard line may be the only thing that will allow the drug user to hit bottom and accept the help he or she needs.

Some believe that hitting bottom is the only incentive that will lead a chemically dependent person to seek help. But parents or friends can sometimes "raise the bottom." Very few motivations are more powerful than the reality of being left without food and shelter.

TODAY I WILL avoid enabling.

Inventory

It took me quite a while to settle down and write a thorough Fourth Step inventory. Finally, my sponsor said, "Just ask yourself, 'What's my problem?'"

That was a good springboard. I began, "My problem is that I always want my own way. I want others to shape up and live their lives the way I intend them to live." Then I wrote down all the ways I'd tried to achieve this grand plan. It really brought home to me how all-important getting my way had always seemed to me.

Before long, I had a lot of myself spilled out onto the paper. Whenever I got stuck, I followed my sponsor's suggestion and called on my Higher Power to help me get on with the task.

Several times I called my sponsor. "This is tough. I'm not getting anywhere."

His compelling reply was, "You don't have to do it perfectly or all at once. Just do it!"

Now that my inventory is done, I'm ready to give it away as I take Step Five. It feels good to know myself this much better. My Fourth Step is helping me grow.

TODAY I WILL use my inventory as a tool for healthy change.

November 21

Let Go and Let God

Let go and let God. For some of us, these five little words carry more power than any other combination of words in the dictionary.

Why do we wait until we have pushed ourselves to complete emotional and physical exhaustion before we *let go?* It's only through *letting go* that *letting God* can follow.

Letting go means a complete surrender of our will, with no more clinging to our wants, desires, or schemes. It means a complete relinquishing of our own agendas, leaving God free to do what is best for us and for our loved ones.

Letting God means that although we leave the solutions to God, at the same time we stand ready and willing to accept God's decisions. We also pray for wisdom to know God's will and for the power to carry it out in our own lives.

We may not always like God's solutions at the time; but in the long run, we understand that God does know best. We become able to say, "Thank You for Your infinite wisdom."

TODAY I WILL let go and let God.

Sponsors

I cannot recover alone. Members of Families Anonymous who have had experiences similar to mine can give me the understanding that I need in order to grow in the program.

Regular attendance at meetings helps me a great deal. But my growth has accelerated considerably since I chose as my sponsor a particular person who conscientiously follows the program.

My sponsor inspires me to examine my thinking and motivations. She challenges me to own my feelings. From her I get new perspectives and insights. She comforts me when I am in despair and shares my joy when I have little victories.

With my sponsor, I can go over a specific problem that might not be appropriate to discuss in the FA meeting. She asks me questions that help me arrive at decisions that are right for me. She does not advise; instead, she shares her experience with me. Best of all, she listens without judging.

TODAY I WILL share with my sponsor or some other caring friend.

November 23

Gratitude

I am truly grateful for my brother's addiction, painful though it was, because it helped me see the incompleteness and inner chaos of my own life.

For years I expended tremendous energy, worrying about my suffering parents, covering up for and protecting my brother, carrying messages back and forth between all members of this chaotic household, trying to fix everybody and everything.

When my brother entered treatment, turned his life over to a Higher Power, and started getting well, and my parents began working for their own recovery, I suddenly had a lot of time on my hands. I had to find a new role as our family slowly put itself back together.

Today I am grateful for the pain that showed us how much we needed healing and how much we need one another. I am grateful to those who work with addicts and their families, showing us a better way to live. I am grateful for the opportunity to become the person I was intended to be. I am grateful to the founders of Families Anonymous and for my friends in the fellowship who accept me and help me grow.

TODAY I WILL remember where I came from, with gratitude for where I am.

Blessings

"Count your blessings!" wisely counsels Fr. Joseph Martin, a beloved addiction authority. Taking stock of blessings is a powerful tool to help us remember where we've come from and where we're going.

Use this page to count your own blessings today.

November 25

A Time for Quiet

When I am not in the depths of agony over my loved ones, I often rush around in a flurry of activity. I don't hear what people are really saying. I don't notice all the wonderful people and events in my life. I just make a beeline for nowhere.

In order to take full advantage of what the Families Anonymous program offers, it's necessary to carve out a time in my day to get in contact with my inner resources. Step Eleven calls me to *prayer and meditation to renew my conscious contact with God.* When I practice it, I find that the time I spend in quiet contemplation helps me avoid agony and centers my thinking so that life becomes more meaningful.

"But I don't have time to meditate," you say. I do it by getting up twenty minutes earlier every morning, making a special time to improve my conscious contact with this gift that is mine for the taking.

TODAY I WILL give priority to a quiet time for me.

If Only…

If only there were no drugs or alcohol. If only I hadn't sent him to that private school. If only she would use her fine mind to understand how self-destructive she is.

If only…. If only…. Over and over, I analyze what I've done, regret the mistakes I've made, wonder where I went wrong. I search for a magic solution to end my misery. All this speculation and puzzlement is counterproductive and a huge waste of energy.

How can I stop this mental rehashing of old problems? The Families Anonymous slogans help. So do positive affirmations. By using my meditation time to consider such questions as, "What is God's will for me?" or "Who should go on my Step Eight list?" or "How many gratitudes can I count today?" I can overcome the negativity of "If only…."

I am so much better off when I use my mind to rely on the guidance of a Higher Power and the program of FA. The time I formerly wasted on worrying can be better spent in quiet meditation on some part of the program.

TODAY I WILL stop saying, "If only…," and open my mind to the potentials of the Twelve Step program.

November 27

What If...?

What if he gets drunk and drives? What if she is out on the street alone? What if he gets upset and uses again? Even when my life is apparently in apple-pie order, I can think of something to project into the worst scenario imaginable.

This is the time for me to use a valuable Families Anonymous tool known as the telephone. That marvel of modern technology allows me to call an FA friend and spell out my dire predictions. If I've chosen the right person, he or she will listen for a time, "feed" me some of the program, add a bit of perspective, and help me identify my character defect that projects doom in the future and keeps me from living in the NOW.

And in calling my friend, I'll be doing him or her a favor too, because it is only in sharing the program with each other that we grow into recovery from the family disease of compulsive behavior.

TODAY I WILL live for today, let another person help me, and eliminate "What if..." from my vocabulary.

Promises of the Program

The Twelve Step program was originated by Alcoholics Anonymous in 1935. "It works if you work it," members say. The program promises serenity and a recognition of how each person's experiences can help others. Through the years, the fellowship's basic text, *Alcoholics Anonymous,* has helped many sufferers find a better way to live in spite of their various compulsions.

Most members' "Big Books" are well worn and full of underlined passages. A shining nugget from Chapter Six offers the promises of new freedom and happiness with no regret for the past, only a respectful remembrance of its lessons.

When we "work the Twelve Steps day by day, our feelings of failure and self-pity gradually slip away, and our attitudes and outlook on life change until we suddenly realize that God is doing for us what we could not do for ourselves."

TODAY I WILL be grateful to the pioneers of AA, whose wonderful Twelve Step program offers so much to so many.

November 29

Blame vs. Responsibility

I can pinpoint many early incidents and ways I dealt with my now-recovering son that might have negatively influenced his development. As the firstborn child, he was the one on whom his dad and I practiced.

We had very definite ideas, dreams, and expectations for this little boy. How hemmed in he must have felt! His natural energy and individualism drove him to the limits as he pulled against parental control at every turn. Our family suffered many calamities.

Shortly after I came to the Families Anonymous program, I had to make a decision. In my Fourth and Fifth Steps, I declared, "I take responsibility for my own mistakes, but I no longer blame myself for these inadequacies."

Struggling with personal problems of my own, I know now that I had good intentions and did the best I could at the time.

Today I accept the reality that I cannot change the past. There is no point in destroying my precious present by punishing myself for my past.

My Fourth Step also helped me acknowledge the many ways in which I *succeeded* as a parent.

TODAY I WILL move ahead without blaming or punishing myself.

Each Case Is Different

There are no absolutes in Families Anonymous. What works for one family may not work for another. Some parents whose children are young adults may declare, "No one ever got clean and sober living at home with Mom and Dad." These parents believe their young ones need to grow up on their own.

If addicts do live with parents, certain conditions are appropriate. We need to hold them responsible for going to work or school. If we allow them to loll about the house, waiting for the next meal, we are standing in the way of their recovery and preventing their growth and development.

Some FA members ask their addicts to live elsewhere, a solution that may lead to the parents' recovery and often moves the young ones to seek sobriety. Others have seen their loved ones get well while living at home; but as one member put it, "It takes lots of program. I work very hard with the Steps and put my serenity first. I have rules, and she knows I intend to see them followed. I'm loving rather than belligerent, but I'm not the wishy-washy person I used to be. Even though she's clean and sober today, I need this program to keep my serenity."

TODAY I WILL recognize that each FA member's situation is unique, and that the program can work in untold ways and variations.

December 1

Needs

Today I need…
- *God,* for strength
- *others,* for guidance
- *myself,* to do the work

Use this space to write about…
- ways that some of your own needs have already been met
- ways that you can help meet your remaining needs and the needs of others

Crises

Most members of Families Anonymous believe in letting a crisis happen instead of interfering by attempting to avert it. Their intention is not to create a crisis, for that would be manipulation, which is usually futile.

Hard as it may be for a parent to stand back and let the chips fall where they may, people with behavioral problems usually learn more from the consequences of their own actions than from countless hours of lecturing, scolding, instructing, cajoling, pleading, or crying.

As long as our "problem people" are comfortable in the knowledge that someone will house and feed them, cover their bad debts, bail them out, and pay their fines, they will continue their destructive behaviors.

When there is a crisis, how can I just let it happen, while a dependent person I love pleads for me to come to the rescue? Many of us in FA have found the strength to say, "Even though I love you and will always stand by you, I cannot help you. But there are many who *can* help. Just pick up the telephone and call a Twelve Step anonymous program."

TODAY I WILL welcome any crisis as an opportunity for a situation to change for the better.

December 3

Be Good to Yourself

At meetings we often hear newcomers berating themselves because they have done the "wrong thing." Some of them want to "get the program" and change overnight. Some even stop coming to meetings because they think they're "not doing it right." They don't feel strong enough to follow the principles of the program.

To them we say, "You did not get this way in a day. It took years to get your life this muddled, and it will take time to unscramble the mess. It takes time, study, and the building of faith to be strong enough to carry out the Families Anonymous course of action or, in some cases, inaction.

"Be good to yourself. Keep coming back, and little by little, one day at a time, you will become stronger, wiser, and more serene."

TODAY I WILL patiently take small steps to "clear away the wreckage of the past" and to live today a better way.

Detachment

In Families Anonymous, we talk a lot about detachment. In our program, detachment is the opposite of the kind of attachment that may be unhealthy and unhelpful for an abuser and his or her family.

We are too attached if we…

- depend emotionally on others for our happiness
- worry constantly, preoccupied with someone else's behavior
- rescue and take inappropriate care of another
- alter our lives in an effort to please someone else
- manipulate to try to get the best results
- obsess with trying to control someone else

We can love a person more freely by the kind of detachment that lets us…

- invest in our own happiness
- replace worry with faith in ourselves, others, and a Higher Power
- stop rescuing (bailing out, covering bad checks, paying the rent)
- learn to please ourselves
- take responsibility for our own lives

TODAY I WILL concentrate on the FA principle of *detachment.*

December 5

How Important Is It?

One day when my son was a toddler, we had a terrible fight. He wanted to put toothpaste on his own toothbrush. I wanted to put it on *for* him. After all, he might make a mess and also waste half a penny's worth of toothpaste!

As time went on, our battle of wills found many issues to contest: noise, the mess in his room, his choice of friends, dirt under his fingernails.

When he was 13, the issue was a haircut. He wanted the current style. I wanted him to look acceptable in my friends' eyes.

Until I came to Families Anonymous, my boy had to fight desperately for the right to be himself, a circumstance that may have made him more rebellious than the average teenager. And what more profound way to rebel than by using drugs?

Knowing now what FA has taught me, I wish I'd saved my "ammunition" for the more important issues in life. The Twelve Step program encourages me to not "regret the past nor wish to shut the door on it." But now I can learn from past mistakes.

TODAY I WILL refrain from pressing my demands unless they are truly important.

Action Now?

Life with a self-destructive person can get pretty desperate. We sometimes think we cannot go on another day and that we must take some action.

But how wisely can we act when we are angry and confused? The best action may be to go to a Families Anonymous meeting, call a sponsor or fellow member, read some FA literature, or do all three.

Suppose I find myself in such a situation? After getting back on track with my program, I will calm down and look for a new perspective on my situation. I can make a prayerful decision when I am sure I can follow through on it. If I am not strong enough to act decisively, I must wait until my Higher Power gives me the power to carry out whatever needs to be done.

TODAY I WILL seek a quiet place where I can garner confidence and strength, so that my actions will be wise ones.

December 7

FA Unity

As a newcomer in Families Anonymous, I was amazed to find many people with the same problems that I had. Some of these people were recovering from an obsessive concern for constantly erring family members. Others were still struggling.

I found myself struggling too. I was depressed by the situations some FA members reported. But I was also encouraged by the stories told by members who were facing life bravely in spite of unsolved problems. Then there were members whose addicts were already in recovery. How I envied them!

Continuing to go to meetings, I eventually realized that my success in this program has little to do with my loved one's sobriety, but everything to do with my own mental and emotional health. We all confront the same illness, even though we may be at different stages of recovery. In our meetings, as well as outside of them, we share and work together. We give service in many ways: being there, making coffee, setting up chairs, and cleaning up. We say *yes* when asked to lead a meeting. We take phone calls from newcomers, helping them with the Steps or listening while they come to terms with life as it is.

TODAY I WILL do what I can to promote the unity of FA, while I work toward my own recovery.

Self-Respect

Living with a drug user has a way of destroying our self-respect. In their rage and frantic need to justify their actions, drug users strike out at the people closest to them. "If you didn't do this, I wouldn't do that." "What do you expect, when you never did this or that?"

Living with this burden of misery, I let guilt destroy my healthy self-image. I lost all respect for myself. How could I expect my child to have any respect for me when I had become a doormat?

Then I found the Twelve Step program of Families Anonymous. When I began to live as I believed my Higher Power intended, I could accept and respect myself again. I realized that what others think of me is none of my business. Inner acceptance of myself is far more important than the approval or disapproval of my loved one, her friends, or anyone else.

Surprisingly, this change in my attitude coincided with a change in my daughter. She now shows more consideration for my feelings than she used to. I do not measure myself against anyone else's opinion of me, but I know that when I respect myself, others are more likely to respect me too.

TODAY I WILL affirm my own worth and respect myself.

December 9

Attitudes

With the help of my Higher Power and the Families Anonymous program, I believe I am finally recovering. My recovery has required a change in my attitude. Now I have a clear conscience and a heart free of resentment, because I have worked the Steps and let their power heal my wounds and me. I don't feel that others' shortcomings constitute a personal attack on me. I take care of my own well-being.

I have almost eliminated my compulsive behavior with respect to family matters. It is no longer necessary for me to involve myself in every family discussion, every decision, and all responsibilities.

In addition, and with humility as my guide, I have been able to move out of self-imposed isolation and grow in the ability to share with others my feelings and my needs.

TODAY I WILL enjoy my new attitudes and the joy they give.

How God Speaks to Me

Sometimes I'm almost afraid to be alone. It's as though I don't want to know what I'm thinking or how I'm feeling. Yet the Families Anonymous program teaches me to listen more carefully to myself and to others. I need to be willing to be quiet and listen rather than continually distracting myself with "busy-ness."

When I took Step Three, I stopped telling my Higher Power what I wanted, and I tried to focus more on what God would have me do. By listening, I became conscious of feelings and needs of my own. I became honest with myself, and this led me to be more open with and responsive to others.

I have learned that my Higher Power often speaks to me through others and also through what I hear myself saying to others.

TODAY I WILL give myself time to listen carefully.

December 11

The Gift of Serenity

I believe that achieving serenity is the goal of the Families Anonymous program. Serenity is a wonderful inner gift that enables me to take life in stride, the bad along with the good. Even the most difficult situations become manageable when I can count on my own serenity. But how can I get serenity and hold on to it?

I slowly begin to have serenity when I try to keep contact with my Higher Power, not just for a short time during meditation, but all day, every day, as I go about my activities. I maintain serenity by referring frequently to FA literature to refresh my understanding of the Twelve Steps, those all-important principles that guide my personal life. Living by the wisdom of the Steps is particularly vital to my serenity.

TODAY I WILL claim and be grateful for my serenity, which is a gift I cannot throw away.

Curiosity Killed…

My recovering adult son lived in another city. He attended meetings, talked with me often on the telephone about his program, and told me that he was doing great.

But some of his statements didn't add up. He was undependable and rarely kept his word. My old suspicions flared up. I thought, "He's probably using again." A little detective work convinced me that, sure enough, he was "out there running" again.

I called my sponsor, who listened patiently, then asked, "What have you gained by checking up on your son?"

I thought about it, then declared, "I don't want him to put anything over on me."

"Do you think it's a good use of your time to spend it looking into his business?"

I stopped short. I had given up my precious serenity just to be the master of my relationship with my son. I had some work to do!

I got busy with my own program. When my son called the next time, I shifted into neutral. After he began telling me what he thought I wanted to hear, I responded calmly, "Son, none of this is any of my business. Just tell me how Jane and the kids are, and tell them I send my love."

TODAY I WILL work my own program, knowing that serenity is hard won and easily sacrificed to obsessive curiosity.

December 13

Spirituality

I first came to Families Anonymous out of concern for my sister, whose drug abuse was destroying our family. She kept my parents, my brother, and me in a constant state of worry and confusion.

When I came to Families Anonymous, I did not find out how to make my sister well. But FA helped me see that *I* lacked a spiritual life. With my sponsor's help, I began to study the Steps, reading about each one and then recording my reactions on paper. As my Step-work notes were for my eyes only, I didn't fret over them but tried to write honestly about how I felt—for example, about what powerlessness meant in my life.

Steps Three and Eleven were especially rewarding. By writing about them, I soon found a Higher Power *of my own understanding.* I got in touch and stayed in contact (most of the time) with that spiritual "something" that gives me serenity and hope, helps me to live life on its own terms, and gives me the strength to let my sister be herself, even though I may not like what she does.

When my parents saw the changes in me, they got help for themselves and learned to stop most of their enabling. Who knows? Maybe my sister will catch on too, but that's up to her and her Higher Power, which I hope she'll find some day.

TODAY I WILL nourish my spiritual health by working the Steps and using all of the FA tools that keep my Higher Power near.

Pain

Sometimes in Families Anonymous meetings, I feel a desperate need to help other members, especially newcomers who are distraught and frantically seeking solutions. I want to give them instant strength and hope and take away their pain.

Then I remember how I felt the first time I found my way through that door. I recall all the tears I shed. I thought that others couldn't possibly know how much I was hurting.

I probably took in very little that was said to me at that first meeting. I just wanted a magic potion to cure my son's addiction. I did hear one thing, though: "Keep coming back!"

It took me a very long time to reclaim my sanity and serenity, but reclaim them I did. Now I have to continue to *work the program* whenever I am too eager to revise a newcomer's attitudes. I must *let go* of my compulsion to change my FA friends just as surely as I had to *let go* of my compulsion to change my son.

TODAY I WILL remember that, even if I could, I have no right to take away another person's pain, because in doing so I would rob him or her of the opportunity to grow.

December 15

Acceptance

"I love you just the way you are."

How many of us have longed to hear a parent, spouse, or friend say these words?

I find it very hard to say this to my son, and yet I've heard him say many times, "Why can't you accept me the way I am?"

I do love him very much, but I cannot accept his self-destructive behavior when he uses or drinks. Families Anonymous has given me the strength to clarify my acceptance by saying, "I love you, but I love myself too, and I cannot live in the same house with alcoholism or drug abuse. It's too painful for me.

"Anyone who chooses to stay sick and not accept help will have to live elsewhere."

TODAY I WILL accept my son's choices and make healthy choices for myself.

The Light Touch

Families Anonymous has helped me laugh again. I was once so weighed down with problems that even the most trivial of my troubles became tragedies.

By taking one day, one step, one task at a time, I've learned to not view everything from the dark side of life. I've learned to join in on the jokes and kidding. I've even started to laugh at myself and the insane manipulating I resorted to in the past in order to get my way.

Laughter heals. Laughter restores. Laughter bonds. Every day, there has to be at least one laugh or chuckle. When I lighten up, I can find it.

Now I use the light touch with my loved ones, in my work, and on myself. It sweeps away the clouds of dread that used to keep me living in the shadows.

TODAY I WILL use humor to bring *light* into my world.

December 17

Listening

My family and I have benefited from Families Anonymous because a friend of mine practiced the Twelfth Step. My friend, having been through the ordeal of life with a drug-abusing son, listened and heard clues in my conversation that told her I was going through the same pain and sadness in dealing with my own child.

She truly listened with her heart, and in doing so she gave me the first words of hope I had heard: "Your child has a potentially fatal disease, but *he can get well*." What important words those were!

Her few words meant a great deal to me. She truly listened, and in doing so she saw that I had given up hope for my son. She was able to say the right words because she had first listened carefully to what I was telling her.

Now I continue to grow in my FA program when I am willing to help others. The best way I can help another person is by listening.

TODAY I WILL stay alert to the pain of others by listening; then I will pray for the words that will bring hope and encouragement to them.

Gifts

Soon it will be Christmas, a time when many people give gifts. I am wondering about the best gift I can give my addicted son. It is certainly not in my power to give what I'd most like him to have: healing in his life and freedom from his dependency on drugs.

But there is one thing I can give him. I can *let him go with love*. Perhaps my most precious gift will be allowing him space, time, and freedom to discover who he is and what he wants to be, even though it hurts me to see the consequences of his destructive choices.

I can *let go with love* in many ways, one day at a time. I can change my attitudes and reactions. I need not cling to the past or fear the future when I live in the present. I can be continually aware that he alone is responsible for his actions, and I can choose to not intervene to prevent him from suffering the consequences of his actions.

I want to give this to him on Christmas Day—and every day of the year. I can truly possess only what I am able to give away.

TODAY I WILL give others the gifts of freedom and dignity, and I will give myself the gift of serenity.

December 19

Spilled Milk

One evening, before we began attending Families Anonymous meetings, the addicted member of our family spilled his milk. Mom jumped up to clean up the mess, younger brother rushed to refill the glass, Dad lectured on table manners, the dog looked guilty, and the addict blamed the glass manufacturer.

Denying, enabling, rescuing, and blaming had become so "normal" in our home that true ownership of feelings was nonexistent.

My working of the FA program has been a slow process of learning to trust that all of my loved ones are capable of cleaning up their own "spilled milk." It has been a taxing process of allowing them to spill as much milk as required and then letting them clean it up in their own ways.

And it's been a soul-searching process of sponging up my own spilled milk as well, a rewarding process of laughing, living, and loving my way through "gallons" of learning experiences.

TODAY I WILL give thanks for Families Anonymous, which teaches me that I am powerless over drugs, other people's lives–and spilled milk!

Just Say *No*

Most addicts cannot say *no* to alcohol and drugs without help from some form of treatment, participation in a recovery program, or both—and tough love from family and friends.

How good am I at saying *no*? Maybe I'm just as compulsive a "people pleaser" as my family member is a drug user. It's often very hard—and sometimes almost impossible—for me to say *no*.

How can I strengthen my willingness to refuse an addict's or alcoholic's demands? A slot machine has to pay off only once in 100 times in order to keep a gambler feeding coins into the slot. When I'm tempted to rescue or enable "just this once," I remember that slot machine. Is saying *yes* this time worth having to say *no* an extra ninety-nine times?

The Families Anonymous program is helping me build my strength so that I can say *no* to pleas for money, calls for rescuing, and undesirable people in my home.

TODAY I WILL say *yes* to my own rights as a person, and *no* to someone else, when doing so aids my recovery.

December 21

Surrender

A refusal to give up, a grim determination to win, and fighting instead of surrendering are three attitudes that block our recovery from the family disease of addiction. So long as we fight, resist, and try to control, ego is running the show, and that's a situation with zero potential for growth.

Families Anonymous teaches a better way—that surrender comes when ego steps aside so that healing can begin. Surrendering does not mean there will be no victory. Spiritual surrender leads to triumph rather than defeat.

In surrendering, we acknowledge that we are not God. We admit that we have tried everything and failed. We accept our powerlessness and our need for help. We become available for God and the working of God's will.

But ego is stubborn. Again and again, it revives and tries to gain control. How can we keep this situation from becoming permanent? By renewing our surrender, working Step One, every day of the year.

TODAY I WILL stop resisting and surrender to a Higher Power in trust and love.

Meditation

If we are honest, many of us admit that meditation is a word we secretly ignore. It may bring to mind mountaintop gurus, mysterious incantations, strange effects. "That spooky stuff's just not for me," some say.

Yet every great spiritual tradition includes some kind of meditation. Meditation is the intentional turning of our minds toward God as we understand Him.

Meditation need not be complicated or difficult. At its best, it is very simple. Many everyday things are forms of meditation: grateful reflection on the gifts of the program, using a Families Anonymous slogan to calm ourselves when things are chaotic, taking time to sit quietly and open our hearts, praying that our wills may be surrendered to a Higher Power.

By doing such things daily, without fail, we discover many changes. More consistent serenity, improved self-awareness, increased sensitivity to others, greater hope, growing trust, and even increased energy: these are just a few of the fruits of meditation.

Meditation cannot be learned from a book. Like brushing our teeth, it has to be carried out daily for its benefits to become real.

TODAY I WILL adopt some form of meditation as a regular part of my life in recovery.

December 23

Laughter

When I came to my first Families Anonymous meeting, I thought I was in the wrong place. Walking down the hall toward the meeting room, I heard people laughing! Surely no parent of an addicted child could laugh!

But it was the right place, and the reason the members were laughing was that they were feeling better about themselves. They were learning to lighten up, get off the heavy trip, and see the bright side once again. How good it felt!

"How can you tell if you're codependent?" someone once asked at a recovery conference. The speaker's reply was witty and quick: "When you're on your deathbed, another person's life flashes before your eyes." The room exploded in laughter, and the joke helped me to admit the depths of my addiction to my addicted child.

Laughter is good medicine. It lowers our blood pressure, reduces tension, improves our circulation, and reconnects us to the joy of living.

TODAY I WILL listen for the laughter all around me.

Expectations

I was my own worst enemy before I came to Families Anonymous. No other human could expect more of me than I did. No one could criticize my behavior more thoroughly than I did. Perfection was what I expected of myself, but since I'm not God, I could never measure up.

In fact, I had an ongoing power struggle with God. I would let Him do His thing if I could tell Him what, where, and when to do it.

Then there was my family. Since I had done so much for them, I expected them to understand and appreciate my sacrifices and total selflessness. Yet all I got was disrespect, anger, and resentment. I couldn't understand why I was so unappreciated.

Thanks to the Families Anonymous program, I've changed most of my earlier expectations. I no longer have to be perfect to be okay. I have found a more accepting God, who loves and cares rather than judges and condemns. And while I now work on my own goals for my life, I allow my family members the freedom to plan and work on their own hopes and dreams.

TODAY I WILL expect progress rather than perfection.

December 25

Gifts

In our quest for serenity and growth, we have received many gifts. But these gifts did not come cheaply. They were bought at the price of tears, frustration, struggle, and pain. To attain them, we had to trade in old customs, habits, attitudes, and beliefs. We had to give up false pride and the illusion that our lives were or should be perfect.

Yet the value of these gifts is infinite. Not one of us would relinquish them today, for we know how hard we have worked to arrive at the gifts of acceptance, serenity, and hope. We cherish our greater self-understanding, and we appreciate the compassion we have for others today. We are happy to be free of false hopes, false expectations, self-pity, and blame.

Our gratitude overflows when we remember our growing trust in our Higher Power and our increased honesty with ourselves and our loved ones and friends. We rejoice in Families Anonymous, the Twelve Step way of life, and the privilege of sharing these gifts with the newcomers among us.

TODAY I WILL give thanks for the gifts that are mine and will look for a good way to share them with someone else.

Changing What I Can

When I'm hiking and get a pebble in my boot, it often seems like too much trouble to stop, take off the boot, and remove the pebble. It may seem easier to continue walking with the pebble inside, but I enjoy the hike much less. That tiny lump gets bigger and bigger the farther I go.

Is that how I deal with persistent problems of living? Do I just put up with them until they rule my life, or do I stop, take stock, and look for a definitive solution?

Maybe I need to sit down quietly and find the cause of my discomfort. Then I can take steps to remove whatever "pebble" it is that keeps me from living life to the fullest.

TODAY I WILL claim the courage to change those things I can, in order to make life more satisfying.

December 27

If Only…

"If only I had…" or "If only I had not…"—I had a terminal case of "if only" when I first came to Families Anonymous. I kept blaming myself for my son's drug dependence, thinking that some past omission or wrong action by me, or my husband, must surely have plunged him into chemical dependency.

Blaming ourselves for another's shortcomings is a very human failing. No matter how often I was told that chemical dependency is a disease, I still clung to my own self-importance, wanting to inject myself into the picture. In my useless guilt, I kept imagining I had somehow caused the problem.

Today, having grown in the FA fellowship, I have accepted my son's addiction as a disease and have let go of "if only." Speculation about the past is only that—speculation. It gets me nowhere in my tasks for today, and it weighs me down with a useless burden. What's more, it certainly does not release my son to work his own recovery.

"If only" is a predictable stage most of us go through. Thank goodness it is only a stage, and thank goodness I'm finished with it!

TODAY I WILL turn "if only" over to my Higher Power. I have no use for it any more.

God As I Understand Him

I once heard it said, "Religion is someone else telling you what God is like and how you must serve Him."

This is not the Twelve Step way. Families Anonymous is a spiritual program, not a religious one. One of FA's greatest strengths is its members' complete freedom to define and relate to a Higher Power. In FA, no one lays down an absolute description of this Power or dictates any certain approach to it.

Yet I do choose to call my own Higher Power *God*. My Higher Power is always available to me, and I rely upon that Power every day. I experience it in the honesty, courage, and caring of my FA friends. I hear it in the slogans coming back to me when my thinking gets panicky and confused. I cherish it in the silent meditation that's become an important part of my day. I recognize it in my strength when I'm working my program well, and I'm reminded of my failure to rely on it when I fall back into old, unproductive ways.

TODAY I WILL remember that although I can do nothing on my own, I have a Higher Power, and through that Power all things are possible.

December 29

Standing in the Way

When I first came to Families Anonymous, I was told, "There is much we can do to avoid standing in the way of his recovery." How could I possibly be standing in the way of my husband's recovery? My constant hope had been that he might conquer his dependency on drugs. I wanted so much to help!

Our Family Week at the rehabilitation center taught me how I had been standing in his way: nagging or crying, clamming up and withholding affection, minimizing and rationalizing, focusing on him instead of myself, taking over his responsibilities and shielding him from consequences, putting up with abusive and unloving behavior.

When I reclaimed my power to make constructive choices, I released him to make his own choices. I began learning to express feelings, to give calm and loving feedback about his behavior and its effects on me, to tell him what I needed and wanted, while respecting his choices in the matter. I allowed him to meet his responsibilities and experience normal consequences. These new behaviors helped me get out of his way.

My husband's recovery is his business. My recovery is up to me.

TODAY I WILL stop focusing on my loved one and work on my own program, keeping the recovery road wide open to us both.

Communication

As my addicted husband's recovery progressed, both of us knew our marriage needed help. Focusing on the drugs and what they were doing to him, we had neglected our partnership. Physically, we grew healthier and more energetic. We wanted that same new health and energy in our family life.

We looked for a marriage counselor, someone with first-rate credentials, a proven record of success, and an understanding of the spiritual needs that are so important to us. This was the best decision we could have made. We learned our marriage was salvageable, but our communication skills needed improvement.

The three-part model our counselor taught us has been a tremendous help, both in the marriage and outside it:

1. Report your *feeling* in just three words: "I feel sad (angry, rejected, confused, left out, etc.)."
2. Report the *occurrence* that produced the feeling: "I feel sad that you forgot my birthday."
3. Report your *want* or *need:* "I feel sad that you forgot my birthday. I need you to say you're sorry, then help plan something fun we can do together."

Using this model, I own my feelings, give helpful feedback, and ask for what I need. But I also acknowledge my husband's right to choose his own response.

TODAY I WILL keep my communications honest and clear.

December 31

Having a Destination

Have you ever had the disturbing experience of being lost on a back road? Each chuckhole seems like an abyss. Every bend in the road seems to harbor unimaginable dangers. One mile seems like five, and ten minutes seem like hours.

Yet when you retrace your tracks on this very same road, everything looks different. The big rocks are only pebbles, the shadows contain no dangers, you get back in half the time it took to get there, and it feels like downhill all the way.

My experience in recovery has been like this. When I was following my son down the unknown road of addictive living, I did not know the outcome and was unable to find my way to a safe destination. Under those circumstances, life was scary and fraught with danger.

When I made my way to Families Anonymous, I found a tried-and-true map—the Twelve Steps—and many reliable guides in the group who had been through the territory before me. No longer trying to make my way alone down frightening back roads, I could relax and trust my Higher Power to prepare a way that would take me just where I needed to go.

Once we have committed ourselves to the process of recovery, regardless of our addict's choices, our road will lead to serenity and sanity.

TODAY I WILL keep to the high road of recovery, relying on my Higher Power, the Twelve Steps, and my FA group to guide me safely home.

INDEX

Note: **Boldface** numbers indicate page titles that contain one or more words from the topics listed below.